BIG RIVER MEADOWS
Eviction from Eden,
A 1927 Montana Tragedy

A NOVEL BASED ON A TRUE STORY

by

W. David Jones, M.D.

BIG RIVER MEADOWS
Eviction from Eden, A 1927 Montana Tragedy
First Edition

Copyright ©2010 by W. David Jones, M.D.
Copyright Registration #: TXu 1-654-166
Library of Congress # 2010918184
ISBN: 978-0-9831012-0-8
ebook ISBN: 978-0-9831012-1-5

Printed in the United States of America

Cover: *Rocky Mountain Front,* watercolor by Karen Ver Burg,
    Bellingham, WA
Book design and typography for print and ebook: Kate Weisel,
Bellingham, WA (weiselcreative.com)

Back cover: Range land and mountains on the Front.
Inset: Iron-lugged tractor used on the T-6 in 1927.

W. David Jones, M.D.
712 Rosario Ct.,
Bellingham, WA 98229
drwdj@comcast.net
www.bigrivermeadows.com

Foreword

This novel is based on a true story. Most of the characters are actual persons. Most are dead. The locations are actual places. The author is the son of the main character, Billy Jones. The names of the characters not in the Jones family have been changed. This story is dedicated to those with dementia and their caregivers.

Part I

Chapter I

Bellingham, Washington, August 2005.
The phone rang only once. Dr. Jones automatically grabbed it hoping it would not disturb his sleeping wife. Years of night call had conditioned him to sleep with an almost intuitive sense that the phone would ring.

"Hello, this is Dr. Jones."

"Is this Dr. Hones? Dr. Daveed Hones? This es Isabella. Your father Beel. He es wild. He screams murder. He not settle down. Can you come now?"

David dressed in the dark and headed for the car. The 30-minute drive to Isabella's adult family home where his father had been placed had become routine. He was driving on autopilot, thinking of all the scenarios awaiting him. The decision to move dad to the home had been agonizing and dif-

ficult. Sister Sharon, Mom and the staff at the senior apart-
ment retirement home had experienced increasing difficulty
managing Bill Jones. The Alzheimer's disease was steadily
progressing, Mom was exhausted and wearing thin, Bill would
have terrifying nightmares and wander at all hours often
falling down, and the various medicines that were tried only
made him worse. Isabel seemed to have a gentle command of
Bill and could coax him to settle and cooperate. The petite
senora was better than any of the family with dad — possibly
the new face or the Spanish accent, or the feeling she gave Bill
that he was still in charge, made him manageable. Isabel's adult
family home seemed the best alternative for Bill.

Bill entered the home just after his 90th birthday party on
May 23rd. The party had been a nice family function and he
actually remembered a few of the guests. The old curmudgeon
was on special behavior and sensed everybody was honoring
him. His cousin, Ross Jones was there and they reminisced
about their youth back on the ranch in Montana. The boyhood
friends talked about the summer of 1927 when Bill's father was
killed. Bill had been obsessed with the details of that summer
ever since.

David pulled into the driveway and stumbled up the steps
to Isabel's adult family home. He rang the night bell and a
frazzled Isabel welcomed him with a hug.

"I so sorry to call you at midnight Dr. David, but he's so
wild. I afraid he will hurt himself or somebody."

They walked together into Bill's little room. Pictures of
his ranch, cattle and horses were on the walls. His favorite
candy dispenser was on the night stand. The old cowboy was
hobbling about the room crying and wailing, "My daddy was
murdered and it's all my fault."

David tried to console his father. "Calm down dad, tell me
what happened."

"Who are you? Do something; my daddy was murdered."

Isabel pleaded, "Beel, this is your son David."

"Where's David? He should hear this."

"Dad, it's me David. I'm here!"

Bill took David's hand. "I guess you're David. You don't look like David."

"Dad, tell me what's the matter. Tell me what happened."

Bill's eyes were wide and terrified. He glanced about the room focusing on the pictures or to the shadows. He collapsed in a chair and started crying — "O mother, why did you do it? Why did I tell? It's all my fault."

David sat next to Bill and held his dad's gnarled rancher's hand — a hand that told of a lifetime of hard work. Each bulbous knuckle or askew joint was another story. David realized that he was talking with Billy Jones, the 12-year-old boy who had just lost his father. "Tell me your story, Billy."

Bill sobbed and choked out the story of August 12, 1927.

☾

Billy Jones whistled "Parlez-Vous" as he hung up the ropes, tarp and blankets from the mountain pack trip. The Big River trip had been cut short by the incident between his dad and Dougan, the hired hand. Billy dreamed about catching that giant Dolly Varden trout he had seen in the river. He looked to the West and the towering Rocky Mountain Front, up the Blackleaf Canyon and over the divide to Big River Meadows. Now he would have to wait until next year to go back to Big River. Billy stacked the dried out horse blankets over a sawhorse, the salt crystals looking like frost on the edges, and hung the riding saddles from the rafters. It was his job to put away all the pack gear. The men were out working in the fields getting them ready for fall planting. He glanced into the corral and saw his new horse Pedro reaching over the rail for a blade of grass.

"Just a minute, old boy. I'll let you out into the pasture soon enough, but first I have to comb those burrs out of your tail." Billy was so proud of his new horse Pedro. Pedro was given to him for his 12th birthday last May; the first horse all his own! Pedro was all white and about 13 hands. The big gelding could rear up and prance on his hind legs just like Hoot Gibson's horse. Pedro had done well in the mountains, sure footed and calm, and he was the fastest horse in the herd. Billy finished his chores and went into the corral to curry his horse. Pedro suddenly went on alert. He saw a man running toward the buildings. Billy watched as the man came closer. Now he could see it was Jack Dougan, the hired hand, waving his arms and shouting.

Dougan panted into the yard. "Get your mother and the car. There's been an accident."

Billy ran to the house. His mother was in the kitchen preparing dinner for the crew. Minerva "Burt" Jones was looking a bit frazzled after the mountain pack trip. She was glad to be back in her dress and out of those uncomfortable riding clothes, even if it meant resuming her life as a galley slave. At least the short haircut was certainly easier to manage than the braided twist she used to wear, even if her husband Sandy didn't like it. Burt had a dusting of flour on her abdomen and a white patch on her brow where she had brushed back an errant strand of hair.

"Dougan says get the car and come in a hurry," Billy yelled.

Mom and Billy ran to the Hupmobile that was parked near the gate. Dougan climbed in the back seat and panted, "Drive to the far west field."

The new Hupmobile raced along the dirt tracks and over the ridge to the west field. The "Hup" was a fancy car for the times. It was more streamlined than the Model A or T and could easily go 60 miles per hour. The newly plowed dirt rose in a cloud as they sped along. Billy could see the two tractors parked in the gully; one had nosed into the gully — the disc plow still hooked up. Then he saw a figure lying on the ground. "It's..."

"It's Sandy!" screamed Mom.

They pulled alongside the mangled bleeding body. "I think he's still alive." Wailed Burt as fresh blood oozed through the cake of dirt and blood covering the face and chest. The three of them lifted Sandy into the back seat. Billy got into the back seat and held Sandy's bloody head in his lap. Mom drove the car to the county road and raced toward Choteau and the nearest doctor some 20 miles away. Choteau was the county seat and boasted a population of about 1500. The town was built beside the Teton River and had been an important Indian trading post but now was supported by farming and ranching. Choteau had a small hospital and two doctors.

Billy tried to wipe the blood from Sandy's face and head. There was a large cut running from his chest, up the neck and onto the face. Billy pressed his own shirt into the wound. Dad was gurgling through the dirt and blood. Billy was crying and pleading with his dad to live, but noticed a hole on the right temple oozing fluid and blood. Sandy's eye opened and he focused right at Billy. Then the eye went blank.

Billy felt a presence and heard or felt his dad saying *"I will never leave you nor forsake you..."*; the same words dad had read to him from Hebrews. Billy knew his dad had died. He didn't say anything or even cry. He began to relive the events leading up to that day. "Oh, Daddy, I'm sorry. I shouldn't have told you. Oh, Mom; what did you do? Do I believe you?"

Minerva Burton Jones pulled into the hospital yard, horn blaring. Several nurses ran to the car and then came with a stretcher. Sandy's body was wrestled onto the stretcher, but it was apparent he was dead. People stood around in shock and horror as they viewed the mangled body.

"Isn't that Sandy Jones, the commissioner's son?" Word

soon spread throughout the town. Someone ran all the way
to the county courthouse to notify W.D. Jones of the tragedy.
Soon, the hospital and yard were crowded with acquaintances
and voyeurs. Someone from the *Acantha,* the local newspaper,
was there asking questions. The pastors of several churches
circulated among the crowd and tried to find the family. Billy
was standing alone near the car and felt someone place a hand
on his shoulder. He turned and saw it was his grandpa, W.D.
Jones, the commissioner dressed in his "banker's" vest with
the gold watch chain draped across his chest. This was a different grandpa from the one he had just been with at Big River
Meadows. He was all business.

"What happened Billy?"

"Daddy's dead. He was run over by the tractor and disc
plow. Dougan was there. He saw the whole thing," sobbed
Billy.

"What did Dougan say?"

"He said there's been an accident; bring the car."

W.D. Jones said no more but walked into the hospital
looking for Minerva.

"Where are your sisters Betty and Beryl?" asked Pastor
Grant.

"They're still with Grandma at Spring Hill ranch," blurted
Billy.

Billy kicked the dirt. "Why did this happen? Why did God
let this happen?"

Pastor Grant tried to hug Billy, but Billy pushed him away.
"I don't want anything to do with God or you either. Daddy
was murdered. Somebody do something!" People around stared
at Billy. A buzz rose around the courtyard.

"It's time to go home now," shouted Pastor Grant. "This
family needs privacy."

Grandpa reappeared. "I'll take you two home in my car.
I'll get somebody to clean the Hup and bring it home. Don't

worry, Billy. We'll get to the bottom of this. I've spoken to Dr. Bateman and Sheriff Armstrong."

Billy rode silently back to the ranch. The dust cloud followed the car and penetrated his thoughts. What will I do without Daddy? Who will teach me about ranching? Who will take me fishing? Who will be my hero? His remorse, anger and guilt all welled up in his dry throat. He tried to yell out to cry or wail, but nothing came out. Then, he felt the presence again; *"I will never leave you nor forsake you."*

When they got back to the ranch, the well wishers had already struck. There was hot bread on the table and a pot of stew on the stove. Dougan had cleaned up the kitchen, milked the cow, let Pedro out to pasture and gathered the eggs. Billy's sisters, Betty and Beryl were still over at Grandma Lilly's place and didn't know about their Daddy. Billy wondered how to tell them and if he should tell them about the events at Big River Meadows. Could he tell Grandpa or Pastor Grant? He decided he had to keep it a secret. Only his Daddy and God would know.

The next morning, Grandpa, Sheriff Armstrong and a group of men arrived in several cars. They went to the field to look at the tractors. Both were McCormick-Deering 15-30s, the paint still shiny red and the attached disc plows were gleaming silver, scoured by the rocky soil of the Pendroy bench. The field was half plowed but one track wandered across the furrows and into the gully at the end of the field. There in the track was the dark stain attracting ants and flies. The men of the coroner's inquest kicked the dirt and then examined the plow and the tractor. "Bring Dougan out here. We need to talk to Dougan," said the sheriff.

The sheriff and deputy drove over to the buildings and found Dougan watering Minerva's garden.

"Come with us," Armstrong ordered.

Dougan got into the sheriff's car and they rode to the accident site. The ranch hand related to the sheriff that his tractor was following Sandy's and the next thing he saw was Sandy's tractor wandering across the field and into the gully where it fell in and stalled.

"How do you think it happened?" asked the Sheriff.

"He must have reached for something and fell off," theorized Dougan.

"Can you explain the puncture wound in Sandy's head?" asked Dr Bateman, the coroner.

"It must have happened when he fell off the tractor or somehow from the plow," quivered Dougan.

"Didn't you and Sandy have words?" asked the sheriff. "According to W.D. Jones, Sandy accused you of messing around with his wife."

"Yeah, he said something, but I assured him I was only helping her up from the creek. I wouldn't do anything that stupid; just ask Mrs. Jones," Dougan replied apologetically.

"We will," replied the sheriff.

The group then went to the ranch house. They found a tearful Minerva "Burt" Jones staring out the window toward the big field. The entourage stood in the kitchen, hats in their hands, all embarrassed for intruding on the tragedy.

"We're so sorry for your loss, Burt, but there's something we have to clear up. Just what happened at The Meadows?" asked the sheriff.

Burt was quick to reply—almost as if she was expecting the question. "How could you ask such a thing? What do you think I am? Nothing happened. I went down to the creek to wash. I slipped on the bank. Dougan pulled me up," Burt realized she had said too much. No one knew about the creek unless Billy had told them. They were baiting her. She gathered her thoughts and waited for the next question.

"Isn't Dougan sweet on you?" accused W.D. Jones.

Burt stammered and then looked W.D. in the eye. "He

treats me like something other than the hired girl. That's more than most of the men around here do."

The coroner's jury excused themselves and left. The air was tense. Burt looked daggers at W.D.

"Got to go get ready for the funeral and bring the girls home," W.D. blurted as he hurriedly backed out the door.

The funeral was hastily set up at the county high school auditorium. The church was much too small for the anticipated crowd. Besides all the locals, many guests from around the state were coming: the commissioners from Chouteau, Cascade and Pondera counties, the legislators and other political cronies of W.D., plus a delegation from the state college at Bozeman. Cousins from Butte and Helena arrived and stayed at the W.D. Jones ranch. The families from Minnesota, Missouri and Iowa arrived by train just in time for the service. It was mid-harvest time, but the whole county put harvest on hold for the Sandy Jones funeral.

Billy was proud that his dad had been such an important and loved man. Why couldn't everyone talk about him like that when he was alive?

Mom, the girls and Billy rode in the cleaned-up Hupmobile. Billy refused to sit in the back seat where he had cradled his father's head only a few days ago. Uncle Kyle drove Billy in the passenger seat and Mom and the girls sat in the back. All were in their best clothes. Mom had a veil over her face and a black shawl over her shoulders. She didn't own a black dress but Grandma Lilly had an extra which several of the church ladies had altered.

The procession arrived at Choteau High School. Cars, trucks and buggies were parked all around the school and ball field. Clouds of smoke rose from the front steps as men puffed on one last smoke before going inside. The 300 seat auditorium was already full except for the family section up front. Billy felt embarrassed and conspicuous as he walked down the center aisle. He didn't look around but heard whispers and sobs as he passed by. Uncle Kyle took Burt's arm and crept down the aisle. It seemed to take hours for the family procession and seating. The casket rested at the foot of the stage but was closed for obvious reasons. Flowers and arrangements choked the stage. The room was stifling hot from the sun and the crowd and there were only a few windows to open.

Everyone was relieved when Pastor Grant stood at the lectern and coughed the gathering to attention. He read about Lazarus being raised from the dead, and Jesus' weeping and sorrow over his friend dying, even though he knew Lazarus would be raised from the dead. The story didn't make sense to Billy, but nothing was making sense. The afternoon stretched on and on with a couple of hymns, and numerous testimonies and anecdotes about Sandy by friends and associates. Finally, Grandpa stood up and talked. He talked about the tragedy of losing a son and his dreams, about the injustice of it all and insinuated that the circumstances of the death may not be an accident.

Billy's mind started to drift. He relived that moment when his dad's life slipped away. He remembered the verse; *"I will never leave you nor forsake you."* "O Daddy," he thought, don't leave me."

Pastor Grant droned on and on until everyone was hot and restless. Finally, they closed in prayer. Billy watched the pallbearers lift the coffin and pass by the crowd. A snowstorm of handkerchiefs were dabbing eyes and noses. He could hear his mother crying for the first time. Somehow he didn't have a tear and wondered if his mother's tears were real.

The trip to the cemetery was a blur. The grave-side throng again heard Pastor Grant go on about God's will and God needing Daddy more than we did. The coffin was lowered into the hole and many people filed by and threw a handful of dirt on the coffin. Billy held back. He thought, "I can't bury my dad any deeper. I've done enough already."

Billy dreaded the gathering of family and neighbors that was to follow back at the home ranch. He couldn't stand being hugged or coddled by one more old lady. When they got into the yard, he bolted from the car and ran to the barn. Pedro would listen and understand. He buried his face in Pedro's neck and sobbed, his first tears in days — "It's my fault." Billy stayed in the barn until dark and all of the people had left.

The next day, Sheriff Armstrong drove out having already stopped at Grandpa's. He wanted to talk to Dougan and found him in the barn. Billy followed the sheriff and eavesdropped on the conversation from the hay loft.

"Dougan, the grand jury felt there wasn't enough evidence to arrest you, but I'm still investigating. Don't leave the county," growled the sheriff.

Billy was confused. What should he do next? His cousin Ralph Burton was suspicious that Sandy died by foul play. So was Grandpa. Should he tell them what he had done? Should he confess and ruin his mother's name? Then he wouldn't have a mother either. As he pondered, his guilt welled up. "It's my fault dad is dead," he sobbed. He sat alone in the hay mow. The whole spring and summer of 1927 flashed by. It was the best and worst year of his life.

Chapter II

The four-car train lumbered up the grade past deep drifts of blackened snow that had been dusted with coal smoke all winter. The fields and pastures were all brown — it was mid March; spring by the calendar, but two months from spring on the high plateau. The passenger car had only a few passengers: A mother with two children returning from a visit to Great Falls, two high school students coming home after a week at boarding school and a railroad official. An unkempt man sat alone in the back. He was a tall, well built man that appeared to be in his thirties. He had several days' growth of beard and was dressed in what once had been rather dapper clothes. The dude had on low cut oxfords, stained and wrinkled gabardine slacks and a collarless shirt. The collar and the tie were missing. His coat was a rather thin, double breasted gabardine with several buttons missing so it flapped open. Dark brown hair stood up in every direction, as if he had slept through a tornado and his penetrating blue eyes were outlined with bloodshot sclera. A small satchel lay clutched to his lap. He certainly looked out of place. The scruffy looking man summoned the conductor, "When we get to Pendroy, how do I get to Canada? I thought this train went to Canada."

"Pendroy is the end of the line; either ride back to Great Falls and change trains or find another way to get to Conrad and the Great Northern. There was a plan to take this spur all the way to Canada but it never got past Pendroy," repeated the conductor.

"I'm broke and out of options. I don't even have a dollar for the fare back," said the stranger.

"You probably can get a job on one of the ranches. It's calving season and then will come spring field work," offered the conductor.

The train pulled into Pendroy, a town that had sprung up at the end of the line only 12 years ago. Pendroy sported three grain elevators, two mercantile stores, two lumber yards, a bank and a tavern. Even with prohibition, the tavern was thriving. The prairie town also had a Methodist church, a hotel with a restaurant, a four-room school, about 20 houses and the total population was about 200. Farms and ranches surrounded and supported the town.

The unkempt stranger stepped off the train and wandered down the wide street. The cold west wind penetrated his rather thin coat and he was pelted by grit in the blowing dust. The tavern loomed in the center of town.

"There may be a back room where something stronger than soda is offered," he thought. As a smuggler on the bootlegger trail running Canadian whiskey to Great Falls, Helena and Butte, he could spot a speakeasy when he saw one. Unfortunately, that job was over. He had been "let go" because some of the shipment had disappeared.

A mustached short man with an apron stepped out. "Can I help you?" he said.

"I'm looking for work till I can earn enough for a ticket back to civilization," said the stranger.

"What kind of work do you do?" asked the barkeep.

"Anything; I can drive, I'm pretty good with horses. I grew up on a farm before I went off to war," he said.

"I heard Sandy Jones needs a hand during calving season. You might try there. His ranch is two miles west and down in the coulee. Big red barn."

Jack Dougan walked west out of Pendroy and to the crest

of a ridge. There below was a wide shallow valley or coulee, and nestled at the bottom beside a small lake was the Jones Ranch. A large red barn surrounded by corrals was balanced by a two-story ranch house and several outbuildings. The coulee hillside was plowed in wide strips of stubble and fallow ground. Dougan guessed there were about two sections of tilled ground or 1200 acres. The bottom of the coulee was pasture where a herd of brown and white cattle grazed. More cattle were in the corrals. The Rocky Mountain Front loomed in the distance—the mountains gleamed white in their winter coat and he guessed they were the source of the biting wind. He walked to the ranch house and knocked. An attractive woman with in a flour dusted apron answered the door.

"Is Mr. Jones in?" asked Dougan.

"He's out in the barn. One of the heifers is having difficulty calving," she replied. "Come in and warm up. You look under-dressed for this cold wind. I'm Mrs. Jones, Minerva — but everyone calls me Burt."

"Dougan, Jack Dougan, ma'am," he said as they shook hands. "I'm here looking for work. I'm stranded here in Pendroy."

"Here, put on this heavy coat and go out to the barn."

Dougan walked toward the barn. It was an impressive building, looking like the big barns of Pennsylvania. It was tall with a smooth curved roof and a huge hay mow. Large sliding doors were open and the mow door was closed. Inside he could see several box stalls, each with two or three cows. A voice came from the back stall. "Easy, girl."

Sandy Jones was crouched beside a small cow lying on her side in the box stall. One foot was protruding from the heifer's vagina. "Excuse me," said Dougan. "I'm looking for Mr. Jones."

"I'm Jones, but a little busy. Hand me that length of chain. This little heifer's got a single footling presentation and her calf is probably 80 to 90 pounds." He looped the chain around the foot and attached it to a block and tackle tied to a support post. He tightened the rope and pulled until the heifer skidded on the floor, but the calf wouldn't budge.

"We're going to lose them both if we don't do something quickly."

Dougan stepped up. "I watched a midwife deliver a breech baby in a French farmhouse during the war. Maybe we could try to rotate the calf."

"Anything is worth a try," Sandy said.

The stranger took off his coat and rolled up his sleeves. "We have to push the calf back in and then try to reach inside and pull the other foot down." They pushed with no movement. Finally, Dougan put his foot against the protruding hoof and both men pushed. The foot receded into the birth canal. Dougan then reached deep inside the heifer and found the other leg; it was folded back along the calf's body. He tried first pulling, then rotating, and finally the foot came forward alongside the other foot. Both feet now protruded from the birth canal and they reattached the chain to both feet and tightened the block and tackle. This time the calf moved and then, with a gush, came sliding out. The heifer strained to stand but she collapsed, paralyzed in the hind quarter.

Dougan and Sandy stripped the membranes from the calf and Sandy blew into the calf's nose. The calf stirred and coughed.

"I think we saved them. Thanks, Mr. ...?" Sandy said. "Dougan. Jack Dougan." The stranger offered his hand.

"I'm looking for work," said Dougan.

"You're hired," said Sandy.

They dried off the calf and put it to the cow's udder. The calf nursed. The cow was still partly paralyzed. "She probably will be okay by tomorrow," said Sandy. "Come on to the house and we can warm up before evening cow feeding. Billy will be home from school and he can help, but first, let's get you

some ranching clothes." They left for Pendroy and Larson's
Mercantile.

Sandy Jones, the young farmer — rancher of the year, was a
driven man. He was named for his grandfather John and grandmother Mary Reid; thus, John Reid Jones, but he had always
been Sandy. Sandy got his name from his light reddish hair
which betrayed his Welsh-English heritage. The Jones nose
and high brow branded him as a son of W.D. Jones. Sandy was
about 5'10" tall with pale blue eyes and scattered freckles. He
was strong and tough and had the reputation of never needing
gloves because his hands were so calloused. He was an excellent horseman, cattleman and rifleman. Sandy's ambition was
to be bigger and better than his father, W.D. Jones. W.D. had
built an empire of 20,000 acres, was a state legislator, county
commissioner and banker.

Sandy had been sent to a military school in Missouri after
under performing in local schools. When the cadet returned to
the ranch in 1910, he was 20 years old. In the meantime W.D.
had decided to divide up the ranch among his children: 5,000
acres to Sandy, 5,000 to Kyle and 5,000 to Wilma. Kyle was
more interested in running the bank, so he let W.D. operate
his 5,000. Wilma was only 17 and getting ready for college,
but Sandy was ready to tackle the prairie, try "new scientific
farming" and build an empire.

He started out by breaking the sod on 1,200 acres in
Farmers' Coulee. He hired John MacDonald and his steam
tractor to plow the prairie. The young rancher then borrowed
and traded to get enough horses and mules to farm that many
acres. It was an ambitious project. He took short courses in
agriculture at the state college in Bozeman, arriving by train
and spending several weeks there. Sandy was instrumental in
getting a county agriculture agent assigned to Teton County.

He attended all the community political and social gatherings and was considered a prize catch by all the ladies.

In the fall of 1912, he met the local homesteader-teacher Minerva Burton, "Burt" to all who knew her. Minerva was a beauty of Scotch-English heritage with light brown hair and blue eyes. Burt was endowed with a buxom figure which she sometimes exaggerated with a tight fitting waist corset. At about 5'3" tall, she usually wore ankle length dresses or skirts but seldom hats. Her long hair was braided or twisted and pinned up on the back of her head. She had a fair complexion with a few freckles across her nose and cheeks completing her wholesome good looks.

Burt had spurned many suitors in her teaching career, preferring adventure to settling down. Her career started in Iowa when she was only 14 years old and after one year of normal school, the school marm came to Montana for adventure. She taught in Great Falls for several years before moving to the Pendroy bench to claim a homestead just across the road from the one-room Mountainview School where she could teach. There were still two years remaining on her claim obligation when she met Sandy at a local dance.

Though Sandy was ten years younger than Burt, he was handsome, ambitious, rich and educated. What more could she want? They courted for one year before he proposed in 1913. Sandy promised to build a grand house for the teacher-bride and they would marry in one year when the homestead would be proved and they could start a new life.

The times were prosperous. Grain and cattle prices were good. Sandy rapidly became a local leader and innovator in new farming science. He imported a short horn bull to breed his herd. Short horns were touted for their better milk production, bigger calves at weaning and their resistance to eye and udder burns in the harsh Montana weather. The white faced herd gradually became brockle-faced.

The strip farming was successful. There had been very little wind erosion since the start. Strips were laid out perpendicular to the prevailing west wind and the stubble was left in place until spring. The alternate strips were left fallow in the fall for one winter wheat planting or spring barley, oats, flax or spring wheat crops. Each strip was 20 rods wide and as long as the field, usually half miles; thus 20 acres per strip. A man and a four-horse team could plow a field in one day. With two teams, it took about 15 days to plow or plant the alternate strips.

Sandy was one of the first to get a truck and a car, which made him the envy of the Pendroy bench. The Model T Ford would get to town in only 30 minutes instead of taking all day in the buggy.

Sandy set about building a house for Burt. He designed a 30 x 30 two-story house with a large front porch, dormer windows and a place for indoor plumbing. The logs came from the Blackleaf Canyon where the forest fires of 1910 had left acres of blackened spires, still sound and tall. He needed about forty 35-foot-long, 12-inch-diameter logs which were skidded 15 miles to the building site. The house was erected quickly and it looked like a mansion beside the tiny bunkhouse and sheep shed. The handsome young rancher wanted a house fitting for his new bride, so he sided over the logs with clapboard and painted it white. The grand house had a maple floor with boards shipped in from the East Coast and gas lights to each of the seven rooms. The house was finished in June of 1914. Burt and Sandy were married in Choteau in August after haying. They moved into the big house and Burt had to give up her teaching position as married teachers were not allowed in the district. The school marm became a rancher's wife.

Billy was born May 23, 1915, just the required nine months after the wedding. Baby Billie had red hair like his dad's. Burt kept his hair long and dressed him in dresses until he was 18 months old. Beryl was born July 5, 1917. Grandma Lilly and

Aunt Wilma would come over often to help with the two children while Burt cooked, washed and looked after the barnyard animals. The glamour of being a rich rancher's wife quickly faded into the hard work of cooking for a crew, raising two children and putting on a pretty face at social gatherings. She thought, "Some day I'll see the world and all those places in Europe or Greece I've taught about."

The railroad came in 1916. The terminal was only two miles from the ranch. Now, it would be easier to get the grain and cattle to market. There would be a town, other women and maybe a little culture. The new town of Pendroy exploded with business and building — grain elevators, depot, tavern, hotel mercantile stores, stockyards, gas station and lumber yards. There was talk Pendroy might rival Choteau or Conrad as the agricultural center of Northern Montana. Homesteaders flocked to the marginal land not already claimed and as land prices rose and a bank opened. A theater was built between the hotel and the tavern.

Burt and Sandy became leaders in the new community. Burt considered teaching in the new school, but Sandy dissuaded her; "I need you to help run the ranch and the family." Sandy was considering running for public office but he couldn't be commissioner as W.D. already had that position and the current state legislator was well entrenched. Sandy had to be satisfied with being on the agricultural advisory committee at the state college and being president of the local farmer's organization, but Sandy continued to be involved in the community, state college and ranching — Burt stayed home and cooked for the crew. She became pregnant and delivered a third child December 17, 1921. Betty wasn't named until she was three months old.

Chapter III

Calving was over about mid April. Sandy and Dougan had delivered most of the first calf heifers. All the older cows had managed on their own. The herd produced two sets of twins, but lost four calves to various problems or coyotes. One of the calfless cows would become the milk cow. They tried to graft one of the twins to the mother of one of the dead calves. The twins' mother didn't have enough milk for two. First, the dead calf was skinned and the hide draped over the runt calf so the grieving mother would get the scent of her baby. Then, the cow was tied up so the graft calf could suckle. After a few days, the graft took. The calf kept his coat on until it rotted off. New mother, adopted mother and two calves were happy. Dougan and Sandy were a good team. "I hope you can stay through harvest," Sandy said.

"I'm happy to have a job, but there are a lot of places to see and things to do. I'll stay for a while longer," said Dougan.

At first, Dougan stayed in the bunkhouse after supper, but when Burt invited him to come to the big house in the evening, he was usually there. Dougan would read to Beryl and Betty or tell war stories to Billy. He taught them the marching song "Parlez-Vous" brought back from France:

The first marine went over the hill, Parlez-Vous
The second marine went over the hill, Parlez-Vous
The third marine went over the hill to give a chill to Kaiser Bill
Hinky dinky, Parlez-Vous

They had fun making up new verses:
Billy's got a B-B gun, Parlez-Vous
Billy's got a B-B gun, Parlez-Vous
Billy's got a B-B gun, see that rooster on the run,
Hinky dinky, Parlez-Vous

Dougan offered to help with the supper dishes and would entertain Burt with stories about Paris after the war. "I saw the Eiffel Tower and walked the Champs Elysees and even went to the Follies," bragged Dougan.

"Some day when Sandy's not so busy we'll go there too," Burt said dreamily. "I've always had an adventurer's heart; I love the Greek classics, Shakespeare and all the English poets. I love the American poets, too. I guess I must be satisfied with the poetry of ranching — the elements and family."

Dougan concurred, "There's nothing wrong with that. Beauty is where you see it. It's all around us. *Beauty is truth, truth beauty. That's all we know on earth and all we need to know.*"*

"That's one of my favorite verses," exclaimed Burt. "Where did you learn that?"

"I've been around. I usually have a poetry book with me as I wander about this great land. I had to leave my last spot in a hurry and somehow lost my books. I sure miss them," replied Dougan.

"Well, Mr. Dougan, I have lots of poetry books from my school days. I could loan you a couple," offered Burt.

"Heavy on the mister," scoffed Dougan. "Just call me Dougan; everybody else does — and yes, I'd like to borrow a book. Maybe we could share some of your favorites."

Sandy came into the kitchen.

"Thanks for helping with the dishes," said Burt.

"Anytime."

* *Ode to a Grecian Urn,* John Keats

Sandy grumbled. "Tomorrow is a big day. I think it's dry enough to get into the fields. It would be great if we could get the spring wheat in by May 10th, the barley by June 1st. The calendar is a tough master on the farm!"

As Dougan turned to go to the bunkhouse, Burt handed him a book of Tennyson's poems.

The new 15-30 McCormick-Deering tractors rumbled across the bridge and to the road that connected all the strips. It was a cold day with a penetrating west wind making it seem like below zero. A wind arch of clouds hovered over the mountains and fresh snow was on the foothills. The arch always predicted gale force winds. Both men were dressed in several layers of wool and Russian Cossack caps. They hooked up the disc plows and started around the strips, one tractor following the other. Each tractor could pull a 12-foot disc plow at a steady 2 to 3 mph. This was more than twice the span and speed of the horse teams. The discs cut the soil and rolled it over burying the weeds and volunteer grain that had grown over the winter. Hawks and seagulls hovered over the rigs, hoping to catch a mouse that had been flushed out of its burrow. The discs would clunk when a large rock was turned over and the tractor would snort and lug down with the hills. By 10:00 o'clock, they had finished the first strip. They got off the tractors to lift the discs out of the furrow and move to the next fallow strip.

"We should be able to plow four or five strips today," said Sandy. "Maybe Billy can feed the cattle tonight after school so we can work till dark. We'll refuel when we come in for noon dinner."

Dougan wheezed. "I don't know how it could feel any colder. That wind is brutal. I've felt a few snow flakes, too."

"This is Montana in late April," said Sandy. "I've seen it snow two feet in May and I've seen it snow here every month of the year."

"Why do you put up with such harsh weather? You could sell your spread, buy good farm ground in California or Oregon and live in the banana belt," chattered Dougan.

"I've been there and the Midwest. Where can you find a place were you can see 200 miles, have the beautiful mountains and own it all? I've built up this ranch and I'll die on it," replied Sandy.

They finished five strips that day. Of the 15 strips that were in fallow, seven had been planted to winter wheat the previous fall. That left three more to plow that spring. Then the plowed fields had to be harrowed to break up the clods to form a nice seed bed. Finally, the spring wheat, barley and flax would be planted. By then, it should be into June, and the strips of stubble would need plowing. Haying would start the 5th of July and last until winter wheat harvest, about the 15th of August. The harvest of spring wheat, barley and flax would start late August and run through September. Then, fall planting of winter wheat in September, was followed by cattle shipping in October. November was time for fixing or building fences unless the ground was already frozen. December, January and February were spent feeding the cattle and keeping warm. March and April were calving months and so the cycle repeated. Glitches in the schedule were usually weather related; drought, hail, late rain, early snow and wind. Disasters included hailstorms, grasshopper infestations, and blight or prairie fires. Nothing was ever routine.

It rained for a week and the fields were too wet to work. They needed the moisture, but not that much at once. The only job to do in the rain was fencing. School was out for the summer May 15th, so Billy got to help. Sandy, Dougan and

Billy saddled up their horses, put the staples, block and tackle, hammer and pliers in the saddle bags and rode out to patrol the fence lines. They wore slickers and their broad brimmed hats.

The horses were skittish after a winter of freedom. Sandy warned Billy and Dougan to be alert keep the horse's head up when you mount and get on fast. Some outfits had a wrangler "top off" the horses before spring riding. Mending and patrolling fences required dismounting and re-mounting frequently.

The ranch had nearly 50 miles of fence. W.D. had put in most of the fences in 1905 when the homesteaders started coming and all the open range south of Birch Creek and the Blackfeet reservation was gone. That much fence required nearly constant maintenance. The snow drifts in the draws would often pull the wires off the posts. An escape artist cow could lean on the fence and pop the staples. Bulls would sometimes fight through the fence, breaking the wires and a herd of migrating elk could tear down large sections. The cows and new calves would be turned out into the big upland pastures when the grass greened up. The fences had to be ready.

The three miserable riders plodded along the line stopping often to put in a staple, straighten a post or mend a broken wire. Billy was the gate boy. He would ride ahead, dismount and open the gate, then close it behind Sandy and Dougan. On the third gate, he let his guard slip. Punch got her head down and bucked just as Billy was swinging on. Fencing tools went flying and Billy landed in a puddle. He wasn't hurt, but only humiliated. He was glad he was all wet so the tears didn't show. Punch just stood there gloating. The men tried not to laugh. They remounted and headed for the barn. It was great to get back to the ranch and cozy up to the big kitchen stove to dry out.

"I need to go to town. Could we settle up?" asked Dougan.

Sandy knew letting Dougan go to town was risky. Would he come back? This was a critical time of planting and he needed a hand, especially someone experienced. Sandy wrote Dougan a check for $30 (one dollar a day).

"There will be a bonus at harvest time to those that stick it out," he said, hoping Dougan would run out of money before he could buy a train ticket to Canada. It was Friday afternoon. Dougan left on foot trying to get to the bank before it closed.

"Do you think he'll be back?" asked Billy.

"It's hard to say," replied Sandy. "He's probably getting thirsty or needs to visit Bessie's place or both."

Sunday morning, they all got into the Hupmobile and headed for church. The small church had been built the year before. An itinerant circuit-riding preacher visited Pendroy every few months. He would hold church in the tavern. After several years of tavern church, the local *nidus* of Christians built a church. The Jones' family had been one of the larger contributors. They had to rely on the pastor from Choteau for the preaching. Now that Pastor Grant had a car, he could drive to Pendroy, hold church and drive back to Choteau for 11:00 A.M. church. Often, he would arrive just in time for the sermon.

When the Jones family arrived at church, they were surprised to see Dougan sitting in the back pew. He had a new haircut and new coat. He nodded as the family filed in. After church, Sandy approached Dougan, "I'm surprised to see you; I expected you to be on your way to Canada or to jail."

Dougan returned, "I was sorely tempted, Sandy, but this place grows on you. Maybe my wandering days are over; besides, I need to see if the wind ever stops blowing here."

Sandy introduced Dougan to several of the neighbors and offered him a ride back to the ranch in the car. Dougan declined saying he wasn't finished in town. "I'll be there for morning chores."

In the morning, Dougan was there, milking the cow before breakfast. He did have a bit of alcohol on his breath, but he was sporting new boots, hat and haircut. That evening, after dinner, he brought out a few packages. Betty got a few sticks of penny candy, Beryl a lace edged hankie and there was a book for Billy, "Chip, of the Flying U." The Flying U was a big ranch about 10 miles south of Pendroy, made famous by the book written by B. M. Bower in 1904. Dougan joked, "I should read that book too, so I can learn to be a real cowboy."

They all turned in anticipating a big day tomorrow. Burt found a small volume of Whittier's poems beside the Kitchen Queen. She quietly put it in her apron pocket.

Chapter IV

Billy was really looking forward to his 12th birthday. He would be able to get a driving permit for farm vehicles on the county roads and he would be almost a teenager. Finally, May 23rd came. "Wake up, Billy. It's your birthday," said mom and dad in unison. Then, Betty and Beryl joined in and they sang "Happy Birthday."

They came downstairs and out the back door. There, tied to the fence was a beautiful, all white horse. They sang "Happy Birthday" again. "He's yours, son," said Sandy.

"He's just like Hoot Gibson's horse!" exclaimed Billy. "I'm going to name him Pedro."

Billy couldn't even eat breakfast. He took Pedro to the barn and chose a saddle.

"Be careful; I don't know how well he's broke," cautioned Sandy as Billy tightened up the cinch. Billy adjusted the stirrups and led the white gelding to the corral. It was a high step to the stirrup and an even higher swing over the saddle. Pedro stood still sensing the indecision.

"Do you want the milk stool?" teased Dad, "or, you could jump on from the corral rail."

"I think I can do it," whispered Billy. He stretched up to the stirrup and pulled himself up the fenders of the saddle until he could grab the horn and swing over. Fortunately, Pedro stood still during the mount, but he was dancing to go as soon as Billy was aboard. They raced around the corral. Dad opened the gate and off across the field they galloped. At the far fence line, they turned and raced back at a dead run. Pedro slid to a stop in front of the family, and then he reared on his hind legs as Billy hung on and wildly waved his hat. "Just like Hoot Gibson!" Billy yelled.

The hay mow was almost empty. The cows and calves were consuming their 50 pounds of hay a day. The new grass was just coming up, but not quite enough for a nursing cow. "We've got to stretch the hay for another week," said Sandy, "but when the mow is empty, we can have a barn dance!"

Everybody cheered. This would be the second dance for the barn. The first was just a year ago when the big barn was finished. Sandy had designed the barn after the big barns of the East and there wasn't another barn like this in all of Northern Montana. Billy had admired his father building the big arched rafters on a jig in the yard. He watched in fascination as the big arches were winched into position. It was fun to climb on the scaffolding when the crew was off. As Billy played Tarzan, he thought about all the things his dad could do; "I want to be just like dad when I grow up," he dreamed.

There was a little pause in the frantic spring work schedule after the spring planting was done. That was usually mid June. The barn dance was set for Saturday night, June 15th. Word traveled around the town and surrounding farms and ranches. Everybody was ready to kick up their heels after a long winter and spring. It was almost the summer solstice and it would be light until 11:00 P.M., so even the horse and buggies could make it home before total dark. Everybody was hoping Jimmy McIntire would bring his fiddle and Joe Hobson his guitar; otherwise, they would have to dance to the windup Victrola.

Dougan and Billy were detailed to clean the hay mow. The dust was stifling and brought out Billy's allergies. Dougan suggested that Billy go outside and clean up the corral and parking area while he finished the hay mow.

Sandy was installing the new Delco generator which he had

ordered from the Sears catalog. It was a large unit so he had to build a shed for it. The gasoline motor was a one-cylinder "popper" attached to a large flywheel and then to a generator. Six large square glass jars held the lead plates that formed the storage batteries. Sandy strung the wires to the barn and then to the hay mow. The four light bulbs gave more light than a dozen lanterns. He also put one bulb in each of the six box stalls on the ground level. Next week, he would start wiring the main house. The T-6 ranch would be the first in the area to have "lectric" lights.

Burt was organizing the picnic supper that would happen in the farm yard. Every family would bring their specialty. The Jones family always brought ice cream to every gathering. They had plenty of cream and plenty of ice. The ice came from the lake in front of the house. Each winter, Sandy and the neighbors would cut blocks of ice and store them in the ice house under several feet of sawdust. The "banked" ice would last until fall and the return of freezing weather. They owned a large ice cream maker that would make up to three gallons of ice cream per batch. Burt always made "burnt sugar" flavor as fruit was very scarce on the front.

"I need to go to Choteau for supplies," announced Burt. "You boys will have to rustle up dinner on your own. I'll take the girls with me."

When Burt and the girls returned all the hands were shocked to see a "new" woman. She had cut off her long hair and was sporting one of those new-fangled finger-wave hairstyles.

"This style is the latest thing and is in all the women's magazines," touted Burt.

"It looks kind of boyish," said Sandy. "I'm not sure what to think about it. Maybe it'll grow on me or grow out."

It was Saturday afternoon and the people started arriving. Billy hoped most of his school friends would come, including

Becky Porter. His three "Billy" friends were coming; Billy
Peebles, Billy Brewer and Billy Wallenstein. Of course, the
entire town bunch would be there: the Swansons, Larsens,
Sprinkles, Brewers, Sheebles, Pages, Porters and Coronets.
The ranch families from as far as the mountain front would
be there; some would come 20 miles. The Sullivans, Clarks,
Noltons, Parkers, Olsons, Pollacks, Sabados came from the
Blackleaf and the Shepherds, Stromzwolds, Johns, Fields,
Campbells and Wallensteins from Pendroy West; and the
Gutchels, Rices, Ridnauers and Torgersons from East of
Pendroy. There might be 150 people. The cars, buggies and
trucks filled the barn yard.

At about 8:00 P.M., Jimmy McIntire tuned up his fiddle
and people filled the barn. Some wanted to square dance, but
most wanted foxtrots, waltzes, polkas or the new Charleston.
Jimmy didn't know any of the newer tunes, so the windup
Victrola would have to do.

Burt put on her newest dress. It had come from the cata-
logue. She was pushing the style envelope for Pendroy when
she appeared in a flapper-style chemise with knee-length skirt
and fringed hemline, plus a silk hose and dainty slippers. The
stove-top curling iron had burned her scalp but she was able
to hide the burn with a cute little brow curl. She was definitely
the belle of the ball.

Sandy wore his vest with the gold chain and pocket watch.
He slicked back his red hair with pomade and polished his
shoes to a high shine.

"You look like an aspiring politician and Burt looks like a
movie star," commented Dougan.

"You cleaned up pretty good, too," returned Sandy.

The mow floor was polished smooth by the sliding hay
and it was almost slippery after the cornmeal was scattered
about. Nearly everybody was dancing. Dougan was teaching
the Charleston in a corner near the Victrola to the tune of

"Five Foot Two." Burt joined him in the demonstration. Most of the younger group tried. A few commented that it was the devil's dance and too risqué. Sandy held back for the traditional waltzes and fox trots.

Someone called for a square dance. Billy thought this would be a safe one to dance with Becky Porter. Several squares formed and the fiddle pounded out "Turkey in the Straw," while Charlie Cramer called "Take a Little Peek." Billy and Becky had practiced this one at school. The three other Billys teased him from the sidelines, "Swing your sweet!"

"I haven't had so much fun in years," gushed Burt. "Where did you learn to dance, Dougan?"

"After the war, I hung out back East where everybody's doing it. I haven't had much practice since I came out West, but out here nobody knows when I miss a step. These are the roaring '20s after all," said Dougan.

They broke for the dance lunch about 9:00 o'clock. The ice cream maker was rolled in and other desserts and goodies were spread. Many of the men went outside to smoke or to take a nip of bootleg whiskey. The four Billies raced around the big barn in the twilight and joined other kids in a game of "Annie-eye-over." Only a few of the boys could throw the ball all the way over the barn.

The feast was put away and the last set started. Dougan danced with most of the women but sought out Burt for the best ones. Sandy danced a couple of dances but was busy talking farming, politics and new generators with a group of neighbors. Billy stayed with the boys but would see the girls giggling and pointing at him across the floor. Maybe he would see Becky at church; otherwise, it would be next fall at school. The buggy crowd started to leave about 10:30, but the rest hung on. Finally, at 4:00 A.M. everybody was gone. Dawn was breaking in the East—only the cleanup remained.

The four Billys had a sleepover and Jean Larsen stayed

with Beryl. They would all be paid a quarter to help clean up. Dougan said he would give up his Sunday day off to help. Sunday morning, the entourage minus Dougan and Billy Wallenstein went to church. Dougan slept in and Billy W. was Catholic. The only thing Billy Jones remembered about church was Becky Porter sitting in front of him and her braids falling down and over the pew back. They got back to the ranch about 11:00 and started the cleanup. They found quite a few empty whiskey bottles and all the plates and wooden spoons from the ice cream feast. The bottles would make good targets for B-B gun practice and they could burn the rest. Everybody wanted another dance next week, but they would have to wait until next year.

Chapter V

Burt's garden was doing well. She could plant potatoes, peas, onions, cabbage, lettuce and radishes about June 1. The last killing frost was usually about June 10. The garden was always a joy for Burt for it was an escape from her usual routine. She longed to plant corn, tomatoes or watermelon that she had grown back in Iowa, but with an 80-day growing season, she would be lucky to have a harvest at all. She dutifully carried the wash water and drain water to the garden plants.

The biggest threats to the garden were the cows. The flimsy fence frequently admitted cows into the garden. What they didn't eat, they trampled. That always brought on tears and recrimination. "You love those cows more than me," she would say to Sandy. The other threats were grasshoppers, potato beetles, rabbits, gophers and hail.

Burt was surprised when she came home from church to see Dougan in the garden fixing the fence. He put in several new posts, one whole spool of new barbed wire, plus a new gate. "I'm looking forward to having a fresh green salad and I'm not willing to share it with the cows," piped Dougan. "My mother grew a big garden back in Ohio and I know how much it means to you."

"Thank you, Dougan. I'll be sure you get the first salad," chimed Burt.

Dougan took a big interest in the garden and would carry water to the thirsty plants each evening. He also kept the .22

handy for the varmints. Burt would hurry to the garden whenever Dougan entered.

Burt couldn't sleep that night as her thoughts centered on
her life. She had settled for what most of the women in the
area would consider an ideal life: having a good, loving husband
who was an ideal father, the latest conveniences including electric lights, a new car and a grand house. She had three smart
good-looking children, but she felt dissatisfied. This isn't what
I signed up for. I wanted adventure, travel, romance. Instead,
I have security, respectability and boredom.

It was flattering that Dougan found her attractive, intel-
ligent and romantic. She would turn 46 this year, a not so
welcome milestone. Dougan must be about 35 or Sandy's age,
but older than that in experience. "I wish that Sandy had a
romantic bone in his body," she thought. Dougan was a complete unknown. He was a wanderer. Was he a fugitive? Where
had he been for 10 years? He was mysterious, ruggedly handsome and quite romantic. She felt embarrassed to entertain
these thoughts.

What would an ideal man be — a combination of Sandy
and Dougan?

June 25th was branding day at the Sandy Jones ranch, also
known as the "Tee Six" ranch. The state brand registry had
granted Sandy the brand after first rejecting the "J". The Tee
Six looks like a reverse "J" with a mostly closed loop. It was
applied on the left hip of the cows and the right shoulder of
the horses. Several of the neighbors banded together to share
in the branding. Billy invited his three best friends to help.
Aloysius Little Dog and George Running Crane, friends from
the reservation, would also come and people from town would
come to gawk. Billy saddled Pedro and Dad took Punch; that

left Wolf for Dougan. Richard Johnson showed up with his horse and Billy Wallenstein had his. The horsemen rode west along the fence line to the huge west pasture where the herd was spread out over the 2000 acres. Some cattle were up on the bench land, but most were in the meadow along the creek. Pedro crow hopped when he flushed a curlew from its nest. Billy was looking out for badger holes and sink holes that were often hidden in the clumps of brush.

They crossed the creek and through the old buffalo wallow that still was a barren dust bowl a century after the last big buffalo herds were gone. Billy had found bones and arrow heads in the clay dust. He could imagine the big bulls pawing dirt over their backs or fighting over breeding rights. The T-6 herd bulls were still in the far east pasture awaiting their summer duties with the cows.

The riders rode past the last pairs and circled around, bunching the herd and pushing them toward the ranch buildings. Billy loved galloping after a breakaway calf or cow. Pedro would zig and zag with the bolting cow. All Billy had to do was hang on.

The herd moved slowly and carefully waiting for the last straggler calf. Finally, they reached the big corral. The wing fences funneled the herd through the big gate and Dougan dismounted to swing the gate closed. They could smell the branding fire, the creosote wash and the fresh green manure. A little crowd had assembled along the corral fence. Beryl, Betty and Mom were there along with Aunt Wilma, Grandma Lilly and Ethyl Briggs. Grandpa Jones and Uncle Kyle watched and stirred the branding fire. The irons were already in the coals.

They let Billy rope the first calf. He picked a small heifer and got the loop over her head on the first throw. Pedro backed up while Billy went down the rope to the calf. He had tried bull dogging calves before but he was too light to really throw the calf. Now, he was 12 and weighed as much as the calf. He reached the calf, grabbed the brisket with his left hand, the flank fold with his right hand and put his knee into the ribs. He then pulled the calf toward him, lifted it over his knee and slammed the calf down on its side in the dusty corral. The object was to knock the wind out of the calf so it would hold still for the few seconds it took to hog tie. Billy grabbed the piggin' string, looped it around the front foot, brought the hind legs up and made three quick wraps around the three legs. He lifted his hands in the air and everybody cheered.

Dad came over to congratulate Billy and to check the calf. "She should be a good replacement cow, Billy. See her nice straight back, her well-formed red udder and her brown rimmed eyes?" lectured Sandy. "Do you want to notch the ears?"

Billy took the notching tool and made one notch in the left ear to represent the Roman numeral V and two notches in the right for II, indicating her birth year of seven for 1927. "I'm going to name her Brown Eyes," Billy said with pride. Dougan reached over the rail for a hot branding iron and put the Tee Six on the left hip. The acrid burning hair smoke stung Billy's nose and eyes, but he held Brown Eyes still. He pulled off the piggin' string; the calf struggled up and was herded into the "finished" calf pen.

In the meantime, the cows and calves had been separated and the cows released into the pasture. They were all crowded against the outside of the corral, bawling for their babies. The noise was deafening. The rest of the calves were roped on foot or tackled by the three Billies and the two Indian boys. Dougan, Sandy and Billy took turns notching and branding the heifers.

Sandy did the castrating of the bull calves. "Do you want to learn how to castrate?" asked Sandy. Billy had hoped he would be allowed to try. He had sharpened his pocket knife just in case. Sandy carefully showed him the technique. Billy splashed the creosote solution into the fresh wound. The steer got up and joined its siblings. Billy tried the next one. His hands trembled so wildly he dropped the knife in the corral. "Wash it in the dip and just take your time," coached Sandy. Billy made the cuts and carefully teased out the testicles. "Good job, son; you're a real cattleman now," praised Sandy.

They finished the last calf at about 4:00 P.M. and the herd was reunited. They would keep the cattle close for 24 hours to make sure there were no complications. The cow symphony had stopped and everybody was waiting for the branding day supper. Billy, Sandy and W.D. Jones were standing by the corral fence looking like three peas in a pod. The family resemblance was striking. They were all wearing their Stetsons and boots. Burt took a picture of the trio as well as of the cows and guests.

The branding dinner followed. They had a big roast beef that had been cooking in the wood stove all afternoon. It would be dry and tough as usual. There was a big pot of beans, potato salad and homemade bread, but the highlight of branding day dinner was Rocky Mountain Oysters. Burt refused to fix the disgusting things so the two Indian boys and Dougan volunteered. It was tedious work to skin all the testicles, bread and fry them, but they were delicious and the well-traveled gourmets said they tasted just like pan fried oys-ters. Most of the women and girls declined the delicacy, so that was all the more for the boys. Billy Sheeble and Billy Peebles weren't so sure about trying a bite but they were teased into it. Now the all had bragging rights. Finally, they finished with Grandma Lilly's rhubarb pie. Billy thought this had been the best day of his life.

Chapter VI

"Is it time to pick the lettuce?" chimed Betty and Beryl. Mom agreed and they went out to the garden to check. Dougan held back, but followed. The new lettuce was up several inches and the green onions were nearly six inches tall.

"I think I see a radish big enough to eat," Beryl squealed as she dug into the dirt.

Burt stood proudly by as the girls picked a basket of lettuce, a dozen onions and several marble sized radishes.

"The rabbits or the cows didn't get the garden this year," exclaimed Burt as she looked back at Dougan leaning over the gate. "We'll have a fresh salad tonight!"

Dougan came into the garden and took a deep breath, sniffing the aroma of the fresh produce. He started reciting:

"And what is so rare as a day in June?
Then, if ever, come perfect days;
Then Heaven tries earth if it be in tune,
And over it softly her warm ear lays;"

Burt chimed in:

"Whether we look, or whether we listen,
We hear life murmur, or see it glisten;
Every clod feels a stir of might,
An instinct within it that reaches and towers,
And groping blindly above it for light,
*Climbs to a soul in grass and flowers;"**

---

* James Russell Lowell, *A Day In June*

There was a tender moment between the two as eye contact was made. The girls were oblivious to the moment as they gathered all the produce and headed for the house.

Burt felt awkward and blushed. She stammered, "Dinner will be ready in 30 minutes. You have just enough time to milk the cow."

That evening, after supper, Dougan slipped into the kitchen where Burt was cleaning up. "I'm sorry to have embarrassed you in the garden. I was only savoring the moment," Dougan said apologetically.

"I'm okay," replied Burt. "You seem to know how hungry I am for a little escape from this routine."

"Why don't you and Sandy go on a trip?" asked Dougan.

"Can't do it now during the busiest time of the year and, if there is a break in the work, all the men will go to the mountains," she replied.

"Why don't you go with them? I hear it's beautiful and majestic. You could be one of the boys," teased Dougan.

The 4th of July celebration in Choteau was the highlight of the summer for the whole county. There would be a big dance the evening of the 3rd, a parade in the morning and a rodeo starting at noon. Everybody at the ranch was hoping Sandy would give them the day off.

"Please, Dad, can we go to Choteau for the parade and rodeo?" pleaded Billy. "I would really like to ride Pedro in the parade, too."

"How would you get Pedro to Choteau?" replied Sandy. "It's too far to ride in one day and you would have to be back on the 5th for haying."

"Richard Johnson is taking his horse in his truck and there might be room for Pedro," Billy answered.

"Okay if Richard will take you two, but you will have to work extra hard in the hayfield if you want to go to the mountains," said Sandy. "And tell the rest of the crew the same applies to them."

Billy was ecstatic. He dreamed about his cowboy outfit and Pedro prancing or rearing down the street. He wondered if Becky Porter would be there. He went to the tack room and searched for the mountain goat skin chaps that his dad used to wear in the parade. He found the chaps, a martingale strap for Pedro and an old pair of spurs. The chaps were too big, but if he turned over the top and put another hole in the belt, they would work.

He spent the long evening of July 3rd combing Pedro's mane and tail and currying out any dirt on his coat. On the 4th, he left the barn at 5:00 A.M., all dressed for the parade. Beryl had given him several pretty ribbons to tie into Pedro's mane and tail. Richard Johnson would be leaving about 8:00 A.M. to get to Choteau by 9:00. The parade started at 10:00. Billy and Pedro covered the five miles to the Johnson spread in only 1 hour. They didn't gallop so as not to work up a lather. He passed by Grandpa's ranch house but didn't stop.

Sandy, Burt, Beryl and Betty came in the new Hupmobile. They stopped and picked up Grandpa W.D. and Grandma Lilly, so the girls rode on laps.

Dougan and the other hands were given the day off but decided to stay home and go fishing or just sleep in.

Richard Johnson drove his Model A truck past the high school dormitory and Teton County High School. Billy was wishing away the three years until he would be staying in the dorm and attending high school. The school ball field was the staging area for the parade. Horses, tractors with wagons, convertibles, bicycles and wheel barrows were lined up. Billy and Richard unloaded their horses, saddled up and got in line. The high school band formed and everybody was set to go.

The Jones' Hupmobile pulled up and W.D. got out and into a convertible with the other two commissioners. The mayors of Choteau, Fairfield and Dutton were in another convertible. The honor guard of WWI veterans led the parade followed by the Choteau Boy Scout Troop, then the high school band. It seemed like there were more people in the parade than there were in the whole town.

Billy and Pedro fell in behind a chuck wagon pulled by a team of mules advertising the Antler Bar and Grill. Pedro was skittish and crow hopped from side to side. Billy was getting hot in the goat hair chaps but finally, the parade started. The band struck up the Choteau Bulldog fight song and Pedro went berserk. He danced stiff legged and reared up. Billy managed to hang on but had to pull leather. People were dodging for the sidelines. Finally, Billy got Pedro settled and down the street they danced. Billy had all he could do to restrain Pedro from bolting away, but managed to catch a glimpse of Mom, Dad and the girls waving. He looked for Becky and finally saw her. He took off his hat and waved it in the air as Pedro reared up. This time, he didn't pull leather.

The pooper scoopers with their wheelbarrows followed the horse section before the walkers and tractors came by. The floats were decorated wagons with groups aboard. Finally, the observers fell in behind and all ended at the city park. The cattleman's association had roasted a whole steer and was selling plates of roast beef with a side of beans or potato salad for 50 cents.

Firecrackers exploded all around further spooking the horses that were tied up to trees, brush or the fence. Pedro had worked himself into a lather Billy rode back to the high school where the truck was parked to get Pedro out of the fray. He was still glad he brought Pedro, just for that moment while Becky was watching.

He loaded Pedro into the truck which was in the shade

of a big cottonwood tree and walked back to the city park. He found the family and got a plate of food plus a big glass of lemonade. He wondered how the cattlemen could make juicy tender roast beef.

They walked over to the rodeo grounds and into the grandstands where Grandpa W.D. had bought them all seats in the shade. They saw Richard Johnson getting ready for the roping events and the Nowlton brothers for the bronc riding. The band played The Star Spangled Banner and the colors flew past them as the seven Lazy P riders raced around the arena.

The first event was bareback bronc riding, followed by saddle bronc, calf roping and team roping. They all cheered for Richard Johnson as he tied his calf in 15 seconds, good for third place.

The final event was wild cow milking. The herd of cows was turned into the arena. A horseman would rope a cow, the on-foot cowboy would then run up and "mug" the cow (grab her by the nose and twist her neck back) while the rider dismounted and tried to milk the cow into a Coke bottle. The first rider to run up front to the judges' table with enough milk to pour out of the bottle was the winner. It was a circus to watch as cowboys fell down, got kicked by the cow or couldn't hit the Coke bottle with the stream of milk.

Billy dreamed of competing in the rodeo next year or so. What event would he enter? It would take a lot of practice, but calf roping would be the safest. Somehow he didn't relish getting bucked off in front of a big audience.

They walked back to the car and then rode to the high school. Billy waited for Richard to come. On the way home, he talked nonstop about calf roping, all the various riders and the best way to train a roping horse. By the time he rode into the T-6 ranch, it was almost dark. Dougan had built a bonfire in the yard and everybody gathered around to rehash the day, roast hot dogs and drink lemonade.

It had been a long day. Summer days were at least 18 hours long. "Make hay while the sun shines," dad would say. Wake up would be at 5:00 A.M., breakfast at 6:00 after barnyard chores, and then off to the hay fields. Billy went to sleep immediately and dreamed of rodeos, Hoot Gibson and Becky Porter.

Chapter VII

The grass in the meadow was thigh high and had just headed out. It had grown taller than the meadow wild flowers that painted the bottoms in June. The wild iris was wilting, the rooster heads were gone, but the orange tiger lilies still stood out like flames in the tall grass. There were about 200 acres of meadow grassland for haying. The yield on the "wild" hay was about one ton per acre; 200 tons would feed the 100 cow herd for about 120 days if the cows could supplement with the dry "cured" grass on the hills, the stubble in the wheat fields and the winter wheat sprouts.

Dad tried to round up a haying crew. It would take six or eight hands to run all the gear and it would take a month to do complete the haying if the weather cooperated. They recruited help from town high school boys, teachers off for the summer, even bums from Great Falls' 1st Avenue South. The ranch was a beehive of activity. Burt begged for some help in the kitchen; they hired Lizzy Nelson, a high school girl from Pendroy. Lizzy would bunk with Betty and Beryl.

The root cellar was nearly empty so they shipped in sacks of potatoes, onions, carrots, beans, flour, cabbage and coffee. The horses' rolled oats from the barn made good oatmeal if they were cooked long enough. Two sides of bacon were stored in the ice house and Sandy decided to butcher a barren cow. That meat would be good for most of a month and they would share some with the crew at the W.D. Jones ranch. Coal and wood for the cook stove was laid in and all the big cooking pots were scrubbed and polished.

The bunkhouse was full and the Indians had pitched a tent in the field by the barn. The four teams of horses were in the box stalls ready to go. The mower sickles were sharpened and fitted with new sections where needed. The harness was mended and the hay sling was spread out in front of the barn.

The ranch seemed like a big factory. Sandy was busy keeping it all running. Billy wondered if he would be able to manage all those details when he would run the ranch. Things just automatically happened to keep the ranch efficient and on schedule.

On July 5th, haying officially started. The two teams pulling the mowers entered the meadow. Each mower had a sickle six feet long. The sickle was fitted with about 24 triangle-shaped blades and slid back and forth over fixed blades attached to the tooth-like sickle guards. The reciprocal action was supplied by a "pitman" rod that was attached to a flywheel. The flywheel was powered by the drive wheel that rolled along the ground. What a wonderful invention by Cyrus McCormick! It had revolutionized the haying and harvesting industry.

The field was divided into 10-acre plots, about what the two mowers could do in a day. The wild meadow dwellers were crowded to the center of the plot as the mowers circled. Everyone tried to avoid the wildlife but occasionally a rabbit, pheasant or a skunk was hit by the menacing sickle bar. The skunks were the worst and perfumed the area for days.

There was a lot of skill required in mowing: perfect speed, constant lookout for rocks or debris on the guards, straight edges so as not to skip any or overly lap the last row and keeping the sickle sharp. Dougan ran one mower and Sandy the other. The best horse teams were also used on the mowers. Dougan had Midnight and Coaley, a matched pair of black

Belgians. Sandy had Emily and Eloise, a roan and a bay. Both teams were steady, strong and quiet. A flushing pheasant or sudden equipment noise wouldn't spook them.

It was a hot, cloudless day. The new mown hay would be dry in one day but up in the mountains there were still patches of snow in the ravines and north slopes, melting fast. The creeks were running full and would until August. Boggy spots in the meadow would have to be avoided until later in the summer. Usually, somebody wandered into one and got stuck. All the teams were issued one get out of the mud pass at the beginning of the season. If they got stuck a second time, they got one of the more unpleasant chores on the ranch.

On July 6th, the raking and stacking teams entered the field while the mowers staked out a new plot. Billy finally was allowed to run the dump rake alone. The dump rake is a 10- to 12-foot-long wheeled bar with large curved tines. The driver sits on a mid-mounted seat, holding onto the reins of the team. When the curved tines have gathered a sufficient amount of hay, the driver stomps a trip lever and the teeth rise dumping their load. It is ideal to dump the loads into rows so the buck rake can come later and scoop up the hay and take it to the barn or the stack.

Billy put the horses to a trot and criss-crossed the field dumping clumps in lines. There were about 10 windrows each about 50 feet apart and 600 feet long. It only took about three hours to rake, compared to a full day by two teams to mow. Billy then went back to the barn to run the hay lift.

The buck rake looked like a big rectangular box with an open basket at one end. It was on wheels. A horse was tied to each side of the box and the driver sat between. The rake was then driven along a windrow "bucking" up the hay. When the basket was full, the whole rig was driven to the barn and unloaded onto the hay sling. A full buck rake would hold about 500 pounds of hay.

The hay sling was a big net, 20 x 30 feet. It had stays at each end, both attached to a rope. The sling was stretched out on the ground under the overhanging track that extended from the top gable of the barn. The large hay mow door was open under the track. The buck rake was driven over the sling, its tines were dropped and the horses backed up, sliding the hay onto the sling. The buck rake then left for the next load.

Billy attached the long rope that ran from the sling up to the track to a pulley, to the back of the barn, back out to a pulley at the front of the barn and finally down to the tractor parked on the ground. He slowly drove the tractor forward as the hay was lifted off the ground, up to the track, along the track to the back of the barn where the sling was dumped. At 500 pounds per trip, it would take 400 trips to fill the barn with 100 tons of hay. Billy wondered where dad got such a long rope; it must have been 500 feet long. Two years ago, before the tractor, another horse team did the pulling. By the time they had the sling back down on the ground, the next buck rake load appeared. The man in the hay mow had a hot, dirty job spreading the hay and getting ready for the next dump. By the end of the long day, they had finished the field and had 10 tons in the barn.

Billy thought what a lot of work it was just so the cows would have a little winter hay. Why couldn't cows be like horses and buffalo that would paw away the snow and eat the dried grass underneath? Why couldn't they all go fishing during the prettiest time of the year?

The crew came in about 6:00 P.M. Most of them jumped into the lake to wash off the itchy hay dust. Dougan was at the front of the line as he had been skunked. The horses were put into the box stalls and fed grain, hay and lots of fresh water. They could eat without expending any more energy and sleep standing up. The mower sickles were sharpened for the next day. The cows got milked and everybody was ready for supper by 7:00.

The crew was famished. They cleaned up the two fried chicken, 10 pounds of potatoes and a plate of beans in short order. They had eaten more than that at the noon meal. Beryl was sick of peeling potatoes, carrying water from the pump and keeping the stove going. Lizzy was learning, but so far not much help but she was good at washing dishes.

After supper, Dougan came in and helped with dishes while Burt and Lizzy got set up for breakfast. The oats were put on the back of the wood stove and the bacon was sliced. Dougan commented to himself out loud as he washed dishes, "This seems like the war all over again, but it's a war against nature, the elements and the grass. Of course, an army runs on its stomach and it's Burt who keeps this army running, not Sandy."

Burt was listening as she stirred the oats. She wished Sandy could have heard it, too. As Dougan left for the bunkhouse, they exchanged glances. "Good night, Dougan," chirped Burt.

"Good night, ma'am," as he tipped his hat.

The next day of haying was a repeat of the first two. Everything was going smoothly. Saturday evening, Sandy paid the boys and took them to town and Billy rode along. The crew had their laundry sacks with them hoping that their mothers would wash their clothes by Monday. The Indians went to the family camp in the west pasture. "See you all early Monday," Sandy said, hoping that would be the case.

Burt was glad to have the house to herself. Lizzy went back to her home in Pendroy, Beryl went to a sleepover with Jean Larson and Betty was staying with Grandma Lilly at the Spring Hill ranch. She strolled out to the garden. The sun was setting behind Mt. Frazier and the whole coulee was a golden glow. Two whitetails ventured into the meadow from the brush along the creek. She stepped into the garden, now lush with vegetables. As she stooped to pull a weed, she sensed Dougan behind her. She stood as he spun her into his arms and kissed her. She resisted slightly and stepped back. "We can't, Mr. Dougan. No matter what my heart says, my life is with my family and husband. I'm sorry if I gave you the wrong impression," she whispered.

"You know we have a connection," he continued. "We both like poetry, travel, and beautiful sunsets. I like the family, too. I'd give anything to have kids like Betty, Beryl and Billy in my life."

"I don't know you. You might be a real con man who has destroyed many lives," she replied. "It's best we cool off and not live a fantasy that can't be."

"You can't get rid of me that quickly. I'll be around. The next pretty sunset, think of me, Jack Dougan," he replied as she ran back to the house.

Burt went upstairs to their bedroom where she threw herself on the bed. Her heart raced and she felt flushed and giddy. Up until now, her thoughts had been a private fantasy. How could she face Dougan again? Should she ask Sandy to send him away? Could she ignore him and carry on like nothing happened? Two other times in her life she had been in this situation: both times, she had to leave the area; first, in Iowa, when Douglas Carver made her life and plans miserable by his persistent courting, the second in Great Falls where the school principal had sexually harassed her until the only solution was to leave and come to the Pendroy Bench.

She yearned for romance, but it terrified her to think that she would even consider throwing all her present life away for some unknown drifter. Maybe it was her turning 46 or maybe it was Sandy's fault. Or was it her fault that Sandy was so absorbed in his work? Maybe she wasn't as desirable as before. Their sex life was almost nil, especially during the summer working season. Both were too tired. She resolved then to try to make herself more attractive to Sandy.

"Wake up, Billy. The sun's been up for three hours. Get those chores done so we can get to church on time," Sandy's voice boomed up the stairs. Billy had slept in until 7:00 and it felt good. He was glad he had taken his bath the night before. They had a light breakfast and left in the Hupmobile in time. Beryl and Betty would be at church when they arrived.

The day was already hot by 9 A.M. and the usual west wind was still. Church was rather empty as most of the ranches continued haying on Sunday. Pastor Grant prayed for good weather, safety for the crews and a good harvest. The pastor asked Sandy to read the scripture from Hebrews 13:5 and 6. *"I will never leave you nor forsake you."* Pastor Grant then preached a sermon about Christ always being with us. Billy thought about that concept. He decided it would be great if he always had his dad there, because dad can do anything. It was getting hot in church so Pastor Grant dismissed everybody on time. He declined an invitation to Sunday dinner and left for Choteau to give the same sermon to the townsfolk.

"It sure is hot and muggy," complained Burt. "It reminds me of Iowa in August."

"I never thought I'd wish the west wind would blow," added Rhoda Larsen. "At least it's cooler in that big log house of yours."

"Let's all go swimming in the lake!" shouted Billy.

They all piled into the Hupmobile and started home. Sandy drove slowly past the strips inspecting the rapidly growing wheat and barley. He stopped several times to get out and walk into the fields. Billy tagged along.

"The winter wheat is heading out. This stand is even and dense. With a little more rain, it should make 40 bushels," Sandy said proudly.

"What about the spring wheat and the barley?" asked Billy.

"They're in the boot," Sandy explained as he pulled up a spring wheat plant, peeled back the sheath and exposed the forming head. "Should be headed out in a week or two with weather like this."

They drove past the strips and into the west pasture. The rocks and holes jarred the car as it bounced across the hillside.

"God put badgers and gophers here just to slow you down with their holes," commented Burt. "Billy, you should shoot a few more gophers."

The cows were spread over the whole 2000-acre field. They were slick and fat. The calves were frisky and cavorting about. Sandy got out and walked up to several pairs. He held out his hand and old 49 came over to sniff. "She's on her seventh calf and still in good shape," bragged Sandy.

"I see Brown Eyes," added Billy. "She's getting big. Maybe she will be as tame and gentle as old 49."

"You have to be patient and gentle with her and she'll come to you," Sandy coached.

"Let's go home, Daddy," Beryl complained. "I'm getting hot and dirty in my Sunday clothes."

Sandy drove the car to the creek crossing. "I think we can make it across if I get a little run."

The car sped down the bank and splashed through the ford, but spun out on the far bank. They were stuck in the middle of the creek. Several curious cows came over to watch. Billy volunteered to walk back to the barn and get the tractor. Betty started crying.

Burt was exasperated. "We've got company coming for Sunday dinner. You'll have to explain why everything's late," she lectured.

Billy walked the two miles back to the barn. He wished he had his .22 as gophers chirped at him from their mounds. It was like they knew he was unarmed. His Sunday clothes were muddy and dusty, but he didn't care. He found the tow rope, cranked up the tractor and drove back to the car. Burt had let the girls take off their shoes, pull up their dresses and wade in the creek. Sandy had walked over to the spring and found the remains of a calf, probably a coyote but possibly a grizzly kill.

Billy backed the tractor to the stuck car. Sandy tied the rope securely showing Billy the best knot to tie. "Slow and steady, and don't jerk the rope," he reminded Billy. The tractor snorted when the rope tightened. The car hesitated and then came free, out of the creek and up to dry land. Billy drove the tractor home and Sandy, Burt and the girls sped ahead in the car. Nobody said anything on the way back.

There was already a bunch of boys swimming in the lake and the Larsens had arrived for Sunday dinner. Burt hurried to the kitchen and stoked the stove. It was so hot she wished she had cooked the chicken this morning and then they could have a cold chicken picnic. At least the chickens were plucked and pieced. Rhoda Larsen had brought lemon meringue pie and potato salad.

It wasn't long until the chicken was sizzling in the pan nearly submerged in the bubbling lard. Burt did a good job on chicken, but she cremated beef, pork or lamb. Billy went to the ice house to get fresh ice for lemonade or iced tea. There was plenty of milk in the ice chest and the pies were waiting on the table.

Dinner was served at 3:00 P.M. Dougan showed up from the bunkhouse and the boys reluctantly returned from the lake. After the blessing, everybody dived in.

"Your chicken is the best, Mom," Billy said through a mouthful.

"Thank you, Billy, and don't talk with your mouth full," corrected Burt.

Everybody raved about the pie and the whole dinner. Before

they left the table, Billy asked, "Do we get to punch Dad's stuck in the mud card?"

Everybody laughed. Sandy owned up to getting his second punch this year so he would work a shift in the hay mow.

They looked to the eastern horizon. Large puffy thunderheads loomed in the distance.

"We may get some rain tonight," predicted Sandy. "I'm glad we don't have much hay down."

All the company left and the dishes were washed. Dougan milked the cow and Billy put the chickens in the coop. They put the car in the shed and closed the barn doors.

About 7:00 P.M., thunderclouds covered the eastern sky. Branches of lightning arced across the dark clouds. Thunder rolled in the distance and the wind picked up as the first few drops of rain puckered the dust in the road. Then a lightning bolt blinded them and the thunderclap followed almost immediately.

"That was close!" exclaimed Billy.

The rain came in buckets. "It's like a cow pissing on a flat rock," joked Dougan.

"It's raining cats and dogs," added Beryl.

"It's raining pitchforks," added Burt.

As they looked across the lake, they saw the splashes of hail stones. Then they heard them on the roof. The wind picked up even more and the rain and hail seemed to come horizontally. Crash went the kitchen window. Burt hugged Sandy as they watched the golf ball hailstones bounce on the ground. The roar was deafening. Lightning flashed and thunder boomed. The hail was beginning to pile up in the yard and drift down the rivulets into the lake. "We've lost everything," moaned Burt.

Sandy held her close. "We're going to be okay. We have the cattle, half the hay and maybe some of the wheat," he said reassuringly; however, he dreaded the damage assessment.

Betty and Beryl were crying.

"Don't go near the broken glass," scolded Burt.

Billy watched in shock and awe at the whole scene. He wondered how Pedro was doing out in the pasture or if Brown Eyes would be hurt.

"Dad, what about the animals?" he pleaded.

"They will be all right, son. They just back into the storm and wait it out if they can't get into the brush. They may be bruised a bit, but they're okay," Sandy said, hopefully wishing it would be true.

The thunder booms became more distant and the hail stopped. The rain continued, but much softer.

"I think the storm has passed," said Dougan, "but there may be another on its heels."

All night long, the thunder rolled across the sky and rain showers pelted the land. Sandy found a piece of wood to put across the kitchen window while Burt swept up the glass. They found the rogue hailstone all the way across the kitchen. It was at least one inch across even then.

"At least it's cooled down," said Billy. "Maybe we can sleep tonight."

Monday morning, the town crew arrived. Sandy sent them home. "It's too wet to hay; come back Wednesday. Maybe there's something we can salvage," Sandy said.

Billy, Dougan and Sandy walked around the barn yard. Piles of hail lay along the barn with many broken shingles in the debris. Billy found a dead chicken that had escaped the coop. They walked into the hay meadow. The hay was knocked flat but still could be mowed. They went further up to the wheat. The far west strips looked like they had been plowed, then as they walked east, the damage got less and the last 10 strips hadn't been hurt.

"I think we escaped with only partial damage. The rain will

be good for the surviving crops and the pasture land," Sandy said with relief.

The only total loss was the garden. Dougan and Burt surveyed the damage. Not a leaf remained attached to a stem.

Burt was in tears. Dougan resisted the urge to put his arm around her. "Maybe the lettuce will come back," he said quietly, "and the potatoes should be big enough to eat by now."

Burt couldn't say anything. She left for the house resigned to never having a decent garden. Last year, the cows got it; the year before, the grasshoppers. Next year, it might a be a late frost or an early snow. This is harsh land for gardens and for ranchers' wives, she thought.

That night she confided to Sandy how unhappy she felt at that moment. "I don't know how you can continue to be so optimistic about this place."

Sandy held her a long time before speaking. "I know how hard you're working for our future. I haven't been very good about telling you how much you mean to me."

"We need to go away together. Take me to the mountains with you this year," pleaded Burt.

Chapter VIII

Haying resumed on Wednesday. The hayfields that had been flattened needed to be mowed one way, against the grain. It took twice as long to mow the field but the hay was preserved. The barn was full and the close in fields had been finished. From now on, the hay would be stacked in the field.

The rakers quickly caught up with the mowers, so Sandy found other jobs for the crew.

"Billy, saddle up Pedro and ride over to the Spring Hill Ranch. Our bulls are over there with his bulls. Grandpa will help you separate the T-6 bulls and then herd them over to the west pasture and turn them in with the cows."

Billy was excited about such a big responsibility. This was the first time anything like this had happened. He loved riding over to Grandpa's place. It was about five miles, over two ridges and through two coulees. He frequently saw deer, coyotes, antelope, badgers, jack rabbits and the numerous gophers. He would sometimes sit on the ridge and watch the whole scene. Occasionally, a golden eagle would drop out of the sky and grab a gopher or a rabbit. Grizzly bears were around, but usually were closer to the mountains. Occasionally, they would find a track in the mud by the creek. Billy got to Spring Hill about 10:00 A.M. Grandma invited him in for some lemonade.

"Billy, you're growing up too fast. You look so much like your dad. You're going to be a real cowboy," Grandma said.

"Dad sent me over to bring the bulls back," Billy beamed.

"I know, and Grandpa is ready. He's out saddling up his

horse. By the time you get the bulls into the corral and separated, it will be lunch time. Don't be late," Grandma called
cheerfully.

Billy admired Grandma Lilly. Somehow she didn't seem
as stressed as mom. She had always had a housekeeper and a
cook during haying harvest. She wore her hair up in a bun and
always had a pretty dress on. She would sit and do needlework
while the men were out in the field or at the bank in town.
There were two of her needlework tapestries hanging on the
wall at the T-6 ranch. Grandma Lilly seemed somewhat frail
compared to mom. Dad said she had some heart condition
that weakened her.

Billy rode to the barn and joined Grandpa. They headed
into the bull pasture. The bulls looked huge and treacherous.
Several were sparring or pawing dirt over their backs. Dad's
two short horn bulls stood out from the white face bulls. They
circled the herd and gently pushed them toward the corrals.
The bulls were too preoccupied with each other to pay any
attention to the horses. Grandpa had scattered some grain in
the feed troughs inside the corral. The bulls went in orderly,
the dominant bull first.

Inside the corral, the bulls resumed their skirmishing.
The horned bulls had the advantage over the short horns. It
was easy to crowd the short horns into the smaller pen. That
left three more to separate. Pedro knew what to do; he would
gently crowd the bull toward the small pen. He anticipated
every move the bull made even before the bull made it. All
Billy had to do was stay on. Grandpa just watched and stood
by to swing the gate shut behind the bull. It took most of 30
minutes to separate the U Lazy D and the T-6 bulls, but it was
done. Both cowboys went inside for dinner.

The table was set with a cloth and real cloth napkins.
Grandma had matching glasses and dishes. Billy didn't know
which fork to use or where to put his bread. They had salad

first. Grandpa had brought the lettuce and tomatoes from
Choteau. The main course was ham slices with pineapple rings,
fried potatoes and canned beans. Billy thought this was the
fanciest dinner he had ever eaten. He wished mom could have
a cook.

"Thanks, Grandma, that was real good," Billy spouted.

"You're welcome. You'll have to come back soon," Grandma
replied.

The five bulls seemed to know they were heading home
and to their duties. Billy and Grandpa could easily converse
as they rode side by side.

"Grandpa, tell me how you got this big ranch," Billy asked.
He had heard the legend before, but never got tired of the
story.

"I was only 19 when I left Missouri in 1876, Billy. That was
the year of Custer's last stand. I walked or hitched a wagon
ride all the way from the end of the railroad in Provo, Utah, to
Helena. I got a job herding sheep in Cascade near Great Falls.
That job lasted about one year and I drifted up to Choteau.
The Indian Agency headquarters were there and they had
jobs. I just got there and they decided to move the agency to
Badger Creek and move the Blackfeet into a smaller area. I
contracted to move the agency buildings," W.D. related.

"How did you do that, Grandpa? I didn't know you were a
carpenter," asked Billy.

"I wasn't," replied Grandpa. "I had seen my dad build a log
cabin back in Missouri. I figured it would be just like putting
together Lincoln Logs. I numbered each log, and then hired
a couple of ruffians to help take down the logs and load them
on to long wagons. I made many trips the 50 miles to Badger
Creek, but the buildings went back together and they're still
there today and in use."

"But how did you get this ranch?" asked Billy.

The bulls started fighting and one ran off toward Spring

Hill. Pedro dashed to cut them off and Billy nearly fell off.

"That's a mighty good horse you have," commented Grandpa. "Just let him teach you and you'll be a mighty good cowboy."

They were nearing the first fence line so Billy rode ahead to open the gate. Grandpa moved the bulls. Billy was practicing opening the gate without dismounting. Pedro was patient. Finally, he got the gate open and just in time as the bulls crowded through. Billy had to dismount to close the gate after Grandpa came through.

"Finish the story, Grandpa," pleaded Billy.

"It's a long story, Billy, but here's what happened next. I had some money saved after moving the agency buildings, so I lent it to a homesteader that came with the first wave in the 1880s. I was working as a foreman for the Seven Block ranch then. The homesteader went "bust," so I got the land, 320 acres. I managed to buy an adjacent claim so that made 640 acres and I won the Dupuyer Creek place in a blackjack game. I was still foreman at the Seven Block, but was given a house and a few cattle as part of my pay. That was when your grandma Lilly came into the picture. She was my childhood sweetheart back in Missouri. She came from a banker's family so I had to be sure I could support her before bringing her all the way to Montana," Grandpa reminisced.

"Had you two been sweethearts since you were my age and did you write lots of letters to her? Did you ever go back to see her?" asked Billy.

"One question at a time" laughed Grandpa. "Yes, we were sweethearts. That was just after the Civil War. We lost everything in the war but Lilly still loved me. We promised to be true to each other when I left for Montana to make my fortune. We wrote letters often. Sometimes it would take weeks to get a letter back, but she always wrote. When I finally had a place for us and a good income, she came to Montana and we got married."

"What about dad and Uncle Kyle?" asked Billy.

"Kyle came along in 1888 and John Reid, your dad, in 1890. We moved from the Seven Block to the Dupuyer Creek place. I continued to work for the Seven Block, but I now had about 1000 acres and 50 cows. Your grandmother, the banker's daughter, suggested that I open a bank in Dupuyer. The home-steaders were flocking in and they would need a grubstake. We had to tighten our belts to start lending our savings, but we did well. Most of the homesteaders couldn't make it on their little allotments so they just left and the bank got their land. I kept buying more land whenever I could and finally put together the Spring Hill ranch," said W.D.

They got to another fence line so Billy raced ahead to open the gate. This time, he opened it from the horse on the first try. The bulls charged through. Billy and Pedro just barely got out of the way. The bulls smelled the cows over the hill. There was no holding them back. Billy raced ahead to open the next gate before the bulls broke it open.

"Why are the bulls like that, Grandpa? What makes them so anxious to breed with the cows?" puzzled Billy.

"The breeding instinct or drive is one of the most powerful. The bull would rather breed than eat. The cow has a powerful instinct, too. She won't receive the bull unless she's ready to conceive, to make a calf. That's the way God made them so they would multiply," W.D. cautiously explained.

"What about people?" asked Billy.

"Your dad should probably be explaining this, Billy, but since you asked, yes, people have the same powerful instincts. Men are attracted to women and women to men. That's how you came to be. That's how the world was populated," Grandpa responded.

"Does a baby come every time people breed?" Billy asked.

"No, most of the time it doesn't. Husbands and wives often

do it for pleasure. God made breeding feel good so people would continue to reproduce."

Billy pondered this information while he closed the gate to the pasture. The bulls had run wildly from cow to cow sniffing for a cow in estrus. They were dispersed over the entire herd. He knew that one bull could breed about 25 cows in the two months of breeding season. If everything went right, all the calves would come in March and April. Billy marveled at the whole process.

"Grandpa, could you tell me about my dad when he was a boy?" asked Billy.

"That's for another ride, Billy. It's getting late and I have to head back to Spring Hill and you need to get back home in time for supper."

They split up. From the high ridge, Billy could look over the entire W.D. Jones empire: His dad's T-6 ranch, Uncle Kyle's ranch, the Spring Hill ranch with the Rocky Mountain front providing a backdrop. He could see 200 miles from the mountaintops in Canada to the Belt Mountains south of Great Falls. This must be the best place on earth, he thought. He watched the wind spread waves of green across the prairie.

An important letter arrived from Delhi, Iowa. It was from Uncle Will Burton, older brother to Minerva. He began by telling of the family news and the happenings in Iowa. Finally, he got to the point. His son Ralph, aged 16, was in ill health. Some thought he had consumption. He was weak and thin and had a chronic cough. Could he come out to Montana to see if the high altitude and dry air would help him?

Sandy was hesitant. He could use another haying hand, but didn't need to play nursemaid. Burt finally convinced Sandy that she would do most of the care if Ralph required it. Billy was excited to meet his cousin from Iowa. Ralph arrived by train in mid haying season.

Billy and Burt met the train in Pendroy. A gangly, extremely thin young man stepped off the train. The conductor was carrying the luggage. Billy rushed up and took the bags. Ralph introduced himself and suppressed a cough. Minerva and Billy flinched. What had they let themselves in for? Ralph sensed their misgivings. "Don't worry about this little cough. The doctors have checked me out and I'm not contagious."

Billy sized up Ralph. His cousin was about four inches taller, but 10 pounds lighter than he. The gangly teenager was pale and sallow but had a bright twinkle in his eye and Billy could see a family resemblance in his face.

"Are you as smart as everybody says you are?" Billy bluntly asked.

"I'm not very smart about farming and ranching," replied Ralph. "Maybe you could teach me about horses, cattle, tractors and farming."

Billy was put at ease by his skinny cousin's humility.

"Where will he sleep?" Billy asked mom. "I guess in the bunkhouse with the other men, unless you'd like to give up your bed."

"No, I like my bed and I don't want to sleep in the same room with Dougan and the Indian boys."

Ralph was enthusiastic and tackled every chore assigned to him. First, he gathered eggs, fed the chickens and watered the cows. He tried milking, but couldn't get the pinch and squeeze sequence down. He pitched hay down from the mow and coughed in the dust, but kept on pitching. He hoped to go to the field and help with haying. They decided he could be the ground man to bring the sling ropes over the hay before it was hoisted up and into the mow.

On his third day on the ranch, Ralph pulled the sling rope over the hay bundle and yelled to Billy to "hoist her up." Billy cranked the tractor, jumped on and pulled ahead. He didn't hear the yelling as he lumbered forward, eyeing the hay load as it rose toward the gable of the barn. Finally, just before the bundle grabbed the track, he saw Ralph dangling by his feet from the bottom of the hay bundle. He stopped abruptly while Ralph swung like a pendulum, hollering and coughing. Billy backed up slowly until Ralph's hands were touching the ground.

Billy jumped from the tractor and raced to Ralph's rescue. Ralph lay gasping, half on the ground and feet still stuck in the hay sling. Billy got the ropes untangled and Ralph fell to the ground.

"That was close," laughed Ralph. "I thought you were hoisting me back to Iowa."

Billy seemed more shaken up than Ralph who was straightening up the lift ropes for another attempt.

"You better take a break," said Billy. "Let's go get a drink."

Ralph coughed and spit, then exclaimed, "I feel better already. The doctor recommended hanging me upside down and beating on me to get the phlegm out. I guess it works!"

"Let's not do it that way again," reasoned Billy, "and let's not tell dad or mom right away. They might make us all go to bed."

By the time the story was retold at supper, Ralph was the man on the flying trapeze and Billy was the catcher. Everybody laughed, but Sandy took them aside and scolded their carelessness.

"I hope you've learned a lesson. Ranch work is dangerous. More people die in farming accidents than in the war and I don't want to send you home to Iowa in a box."

Ralph seemed to improve from that moment on. He ate like he had years of catching up to do. He starting tanning in the high altitude sunshine and seemed to be coughing less.

"If we get done with the haying on time, dad promised to take us on a horse pack trip to Big River," Billy announced to Ralph. "We've got to get to work."

Ralph pitched in and, although he wasn't as strong as Billy, he was a good worker. He practiced riding any time he could.

Billy couldn't wait to take Ralph on a snipe hunt. He started talking about snipe hunting and recruited the rest of the haying crew to talk it up. Sandy told him he would give him a dollar for every snipe and Burt promised to make snipe pie for everybody. They had to wait for the dark of the moon which was one week away.

Finally, the night arrived. Billy, Sandy, Dougan, Bob and Jimmy took Ralph out to the west pasture. They stationed him in a patch of tall grass and helped him spread out his gunny sack with the mouth propped open. His lantern was trimmed just right and he lay behind the sack. He had practiced his snipe call all week and could make the high pitched peep-peep almost as good as Billy's.

When Ralph was well situated, the others fanned out down the meadow to herd the snipe toward Ralph. It was now about 11:00 P.M. At 3:00 A.M., Ralph stumbled into the bunkhouse, empty sack in hand to find all his "buddies" soundly asleep. At the breakfast table, not a word of the hunt was mentioned but Ralph couldn't wait to take the next "dude" snipe hunting.

The haying in the upper field was coming along well. Much of the hail flattened grass was standing up and the mowers could mow two directions. The "bread loaf" stacks of hay were growing. They were made by piling up the hay with a stacker. The stacker was a scaffolding with a hinged arm attached to a basket that threw the hay overhead on to the pile. The stack was built about 20 feet wide, 15 feet high and as long as the stack yard. Billy was back at running the dump rake and the stacker. Another hand stood on top of the stack and leveled the pile.

Sandy complemented the crew. "If you keep this up, we'll be through by the first of August."

Billy knew that meant they would be going on a pack trip to the mountains. He had been two times before; the first when he was nine, and again last year. This time, he would ride Pedro.

That evening when the crew came in, the sky over the mountains had a hazy appearance. As the sun set, the whole sky turned red. "There must be a forest fire somewhere to the west," Sandy predicted. "In 1910, the fires kept the sky red and hazy all summer. You could smell the smoke all the way to North Dakota."

After dinner, Burt walked alone to the crest of the hill behind the ranch house. The sky blazed red and the sun was a red disc above the silhouette of the mountains. She also remembered the summer of 1910. That was the year she had so much difficulty with the high school superintendent in Great Falls. Why are men so much like the bulls in the herd, she thought. She also remembered Dougan's words as she watched the sun sink behind the mountains and the red change to lavender to purple. It was beautiful in a frightening way. So was the thought of Dougan. He was romantic, passably handsome and a bit dangerous. As much as she tried, she couldn't stop thinking of him.

That night, Sandy touched her and asked, "Are you serious about going to the mountains on a pack trip? You've never done anything like that before. You don't ride horses."

"Of course I'm serious. It would be a time away from the worries of the ranch and a time to be with you," she replied.

"It could be tough on you; sleeping on the ground, spending hours horseback, eating camp food," he cautioned.

"I learned to be a ranch wife, didn't I? I can learn to be a horsewoman, too," she said somewhat sarcastically.

"We'll have to get you riding before we leave, then," he said.

"I think Judy would be a good horse for you. She's older and gentle and has been to the mountains many times. I'll have Dougan get her ready."

They heard on the crystal radio that the forest fire was near Kalispell was not a threat to their mountain trip. Everybody was talking about the trip. Who would go? Who would stay for the chores? Which route would they take? Would they get all the way to Big River? The hay crew worked extra hard. The summer fallow crew worked long hours and it looked like the trip would happen.

The morning of July 23rd, they awoke to the smell of smoke. It was rising from the west between the ranch and the mountains. "There's a range fire," shouted Sandy. "It looks like it may be headed our way." The west wind was pushing the fire toward the Jones' ranches and Pendroy. Sandy gave a job to the entire crew. Buckets of water and burlap bags were loaded into the truck along with shovels and pick axes.

Sandy and Dougan hitched the disc plows to the tractors and headed west; people from Pendroy and the surrounding ranches came too. Sandy told Burt to be ready to drive to Choteau with the girls if the fire should come down the coulee.

It didn't take long to find the fire. It had started near the Parker ranch and had burned several thousand acres. Tractors with plows were trying to plow a fire line ahead of the flame. Billy and the crew were there with their shovels and wet gunny sacks trying to beat out any flames that had jumped the line.

The flames licked the frame of the tractor as the plows threw dirt on the embers. The fire was burning several hay-stacks on the Olson ranch, but had missed the ranch build-ings. The racing inferno burned all the way to the county road. Everybody hoped the road would stop the advance. Thirty or forty men with shovels and blankets fanned out beyond the road to stamp out the wind blown embers.

"I think we've got it stopped," agreed the men. "Now just mop up the hot spots before the wind whips them up again."

Billy looked at the huge black blanket on the ground almost as far as he could see. Spires of smoke rose from the smoldering cow chips or fence posts like the chimneys of a large underground city. He and his friends went from one to the next shoveling dirt or stomping the embers.

Finally, at about 4 P.M., they decided most of the fighters could leave. Billy was black with soot; he couldn't wait to get to the lake and most of the fighters also headed for the lake. Dougan volunteered to stay and watch the fire. Someone would bring him some dinner.

Burt had pitchers of lemonade and ice water sitting out for all the crew and others that came to wash off in the lake. They looked like a troop in blackface. Lizzy and Burt had cooked a huge amount of food ready to take to the fire line if needed, but instead everybody had a picnic by the lake.

Sandy said a blessing, thanking God for sparing lives and livestock. They were thankful the fire had spared the T-6, but were already planning how to get some extra hay and pasture for the Olsons and the Parkers.

Burt packed a dinner bucket and a big jar of lemonade for Dougan. Billy volunteered to ride along. Burt drove the car westward along the county road that had been the skid road for the logs that built her house. That seemed such a long time ago. She had been so excited and in love during the construction phase. Sandy seemed to have plenty of time for her then and her for him. Their lives had become so complicated and also routine.

They crested the dry fork ridge and saw the blackened prairie extending most of the way to the mountains. The smoke had cleared, but the smell of burning dung lingered.

Billy told his mom all about fighting the fire and how he had put out hundreds of spot fires. They wondered how the fire started; there hadn't been a lightning storm that night, so that meant it was probably a tossed cigarette or a campfire left unattended. They got to the tractor. Dougan was resting against the back wheel.

"Mighty good to see you two," Dougan exhaled. "I'm powerfully thirsty and hungry."

"We've got the remedy for that," Burt said cheerfully. "First, wash up with this water and burlap bag. You look like a coal miner."

Dougan's white eyes stood out from his smeared and blackened face. Dried sweat rivulets tracked his brow and there were even darker rings around his nostrils where black smoke collected. He coughed several times and raised black phlegm which he spit on a smoldering dung hill. He wiped his face, head arms and hands on the wet burlap bag, rinsed off and washed again.

"That feels good," he exclaimed. "Let's get out of the wind."

They sat on the lee running board of the Hupmobile. Dougan drank and ate like this was his last meal. They looked across the blackened prairie. The sun was setting and a few glowing clumps stood out from the black background.

"It's kind of pretty," commented Dougan. "Like jewels lying on a black velvet blanket."

"You could make the devil romantic and beautiful," Burt said sarcastically. "This disaster could have destroyed the whole T-6."

"*Truth is beauty, beauty is truth,*" Dougan quoted. "Why don't you two stay here and watch the fire and the stars with me."

"We have to get back; 5:00 A.M. comes early and it's already 11:00 P.M.," said Burt. "Billy's bedtime has long passed."

They said goodbye. Dougan thought he would be home with the tractor and plow some time mid morning if the fire didn't flare up. On the way back home, Billy murmured, "Mom, you kind of like him, don't you?"

"He's nice and a good worker, but we don't know much about him. I think he has a colorful past," returned Burt.

"I like him," said Billy. "He knows a lot about the world. Not as much as Dad, but different things."

"That's what makes him intriguing. Maybe someday we'll find out what he's running from," said Burt wistfully.

The night was short, but even shorter for Burt. She thought about the evening and Billy's impressions of Dougan. It was a bittersweet moment as she knew Dougan would be off again come fall.

Dougan motored in about 11:00 A.M. and headed straight for the lake to bathe. He went in clothes and all and then removed shirt, trousers and boots as he stood in the water. Betty and Beryl came over to see what was happening.

"Would one of you girls get me a bar of soap?" yelled Dougan.

Beryl ran after some soap while Betty stayed at the shore. "How did you get so dirty, Mr. Dougan?" she asked.

"Been fighting fire and breathing smoke. It's a dirty job."

Beryl came back with the soap. "It's Ivory; it floats," she called as she threw the bar at Dougan. Dougan lathered up and also washed out his clothes. He called to the girls. "You two better go inside the house while I get out and go to the bunkhouse to put on dry clothes."

Burt watched from the house as Dougan sloshed out of the lake, boots and clothes in hand. He checked for leeches, gathered up his wet clothes and headed for the bunkhouse. Burt noticed his lean, muscular body. She also saw a tattoo on his shoulder and wondered about the story behind it — another part of the intrigue.

It was almost noon and the hay crew would be there any time. She hustled to get the table set. Lizzy and Beryl were slicing the bread, pouring the milk or water and setting the long table. Dougan came in with clean clothes and a shaven face. He set up the wash stand by the back door and pumped a bucket of water for drinking or washing.

"I'll bet you're ready for a nap," said Burt.

"First dinner, then a nap. A bath used to be first on the list, but I fixed that," he laughed.

The crew came in. Billy was first at the wash basin followed by Ralph Burton, Dave Duncan and the two Indians. Sandy came last.

Billy asked Dougan, "How was it up at the fire line all night?"

Dougan drew out his response. "I only had to fight off two grizzlies and a pack of coyotes. They were out there looking for roasted meat. Seriously, it was kind of boring. I did make up a poem about it. Come to the bunkhouse tonight and hear it."

They went back to the hay fields after dinner. It was threatening rain so they worked late to get as much hay in as possible. The best hay had been cut. Now, they were mowing the thinner hay on the hillsides or trying to mow the wet spots or bogs that had dried out in the last few weeks. Haying would soon be finished. After dinner, Billy went to the bunkhouse to hear Dougan's poem. Dougan gathered the boys around.

"You know what the most aggravating thing about this place is?" he asked. He answered his own question. "The wind. That persistent, west wind."

> *Where does the wind go when it doesn't blow,*
> *the cowboy asked his friend?*
> *There's a cave on Blackleaf Mountain*
> *where the weather has its den.*
> *And there it schemes and plans what trick it next will do,*
> *To rain or snow or sleet or blow and make a fool of you.*

It loves to scatter windrows and chase the clouds at play,
Or steal your hat in nothin' flat and blow it far away.
It's violent and vicious when it drives the hammering hail,
Or fans the fire to a funeral pyre and blows it down the vail.
I never heard of wind chill; that's the weatherman's invention,
But the old West wind can cut through skin
*   and freeze you without question.*
See that no eared bobtailed cow; the wind has got her branded,
That flattened shed, that bare seed bed,
*   that tree that's been upended.*
The drifts pile high and block the roads;
*   hurray, they've cancelled school,*
The hills swept bare, there's grass up there;
*   the cows will have some fuel.*
But if perchance that old West wind
*   would take a minutes' rest,*
*We'd say a prayer 'gainst stagnant air and all fall to the West.**

"That's great," laughed Billy. "Write it down, so I can show it to Mom. She'll like it!"

---

* *The West Wind,* by the author.

Chapter IX

"If Mom's going to the mountains with us, we have to teach her to ride," Sandy said to Billy. "Why don't you take her for a ride? Saddle up Judy with that small saddle, shorten up the stirrups and ride to Pendroy."

Billy was excited to take mom for a ride. Mom had so far declined to have much to do with horses, tractors or field work. She reasoned rightly that she might be drafted for a ranch hand. She didn't even own a pair of pants. Billy ran to the house.

"Mom, let's go for a horseback ride. You need to get ready to go on a mountain pack trip. We'll have fun," coaxed Billy.

Burt reluctantly agreed. It had been years since she had ridden a horse and she was nervous about it. She thought about what she would wear. Billy was now just her height but she wouldn't fit his pants. Maybe she could alter Sandy's pants so she tried several pairs on until one almost fit. It was okay in the waist and thighs, but tight across the seat. They could be altered later. She found a shirt and could wear her gardening hat. Billy's boots were too narrow, but okay for length. She looked like a war refugee as she hobbled to the barn.

Billy brought the horses into the corral. He checked the stirrup length and then tried to give Mom a foot up. She missed the stirrup and they both fell into the corral dirt laughing.

"Do you want me to get a stool?" asked Billy.

"Let's try it again. This time I'll be more careful," said Burt nervously.

"Put your foot in my hands, grab the saddle horn and swing your right leg over the horse. Then put your left foot in the stirrup I'll hand you your reins when you're aboard," said Billy confidently.

This time, she got the leg across but couldn't get the left foot into the stirrup. Billy pushed and finally got her into the saddle, then the feet into the stirrups. Judy patiently tolerated the production.

"I'm glad we didn't have an audience," said Burt, "I think I popped the seat seam in Dad's pants."

Billy tried hard not to laugh. "You're doing great, mom. Let's ride around in the corral a few times."

The two riders circled the corral several times. Burt squirmed to find a comfortable position. She really felt awkward. Judy plodded steadily around the corral.

"Are you ready to hit the trail?" asked Billy.

"Ready as I'll ever be, son."

The trail to Pendroy was about two miles long, over the creek, across a meadow and then along the wheat strips to the crest of the coulee rim. From there, it was another mile to the town. There were no badger holes, big rocks or mud puddles to navigate — just an easy ride.

"Just follow Pedro," Billy yelled back to Burt. "Judy is a good follower. That's what she will do in the mountains."

When they got to the top of the hill, Burt was feeling more confident.

"It's coming back," she said. "I used to ride our plow horse back in Iowa. We could get three of us on him at once; Gertie, Elizabeth and Minerva. We would get him up to the yard fence and climb on. We didn't have a saddle so rode bareback. If one fell off, there was no getting back on unless we had a fence. Which reminds me, Billy, I better not get off in Pendroy. We looked pretty awkward on that last attempt, and besides, my seat is ripped out."

"Okay, mom, I can get off and go to the store if there's anything you need."

They got to Pendroy and were about to turn around when Rhoda Larson came out of the store.

"It looks like Billy and the scarecrow," laughed Rhoda. "Is that you, Burt? I didn't think I'd ever see you horseback."

"Rhoda, have you got any decent horse riding clothes?" asked Burt.

"I think we've got an outfit for you. Come on in and get fitted," called Rhoda.

"I'll be back with the car," said Burt, "probably tomorrow."

They rode back to the ranch. Burt was getting progressively uncomfortable. She was chafing from ankle to ankle.

"How do you keep from getting saddle sore?" asked Burt.

Billy had to think a moment about what seemed to come naturally. "Try to support some of the weight on your feet and on your seat. Sway when the horse sways and not against her. Bend your knees a little," he said pretending to be an expert.

Burt now understood why Sandy had not come with them. It would have been doubly embarrassing for Sandy to have witnessed the mounting spectacle and she knew she would have thrown in the towel and walked away.

The next day, she drove to Pendroy. Rhoda Larson had picked out some gear for Burt. Rhoda was a pretty good seamstress and did alterations too. They found a suitable pair of pants that fit most places. The waist was loose but easily fitted. They found a pair of ladies lace up boots that fit and a white hat with a chin strap.

"I think this would look nice with one of your long sleeved blouses," commented Rhoda. "You have to look a little feminine. You could wear that little black bow at the neck, too."

"Who is going?" asked Rhoda.

"It looks like Sandy, Billy, W.D., Kyle, my nephew Ralph Burton and me," said Burt.

"Who's doing the cooking and cleaning, Burt? I think that is why they asked you along. You're crazy to go."

"I hadn't thought about it," said Burt, "but they always managed without me before."

I'll bet they took W.D.'s cook," guessed Rhoda. "Don't let them turn you into the camp slave."

"That's good advice. I'll have to get things understood from the beginning."

That evening, they sat around the table and planned the pack trip.

"It will take a couple of days to shoe all those horses and a couple of them will be really hard to shoe. I'll bet we have to throw Paint and Rascal," said Billy.

Dougan asked, "Who will be the cook and wrangler?"

"I thought we could all take turns," said Sandy.

"I would be your cook and wrangler," volunteered Dougan. "You haven't tasted my cooking, but in one of my former lives I was a cook."

"What haven't you done?" asked Billy.

"I haven't been on a pack trip to the mountains," said Dougan. "It would be a great experience."

"Who would take care of the animals and chores at home?" wondered Billy.

"I could do that," said Jack Peebles, "I could use a little extra pay."

Sandy responded, "I guess that will be okay. You sure you can cook, Dougan? Maybe you want to poison all of us."

"We expect some French cooking — you being in France and all," came Burt's voice from the kitchen.

"You laugh now, but you'll see," quipped Dougan.

"Today is August 1," said Sandy. "We should leave on August 6 and be back by August 15. That only gives us five days to get ready. Dougan, get your grocery list together. Billy, you and Ralph are responsible for the gear. Burt can put together bed rolls for the family. The rest of you are on your own.

What are you going to do, Dad?" asked Billy.

"Shoe the horses, buy the groceries, fix the equipment and keep all you slow pokes moving," fired off Sandy. "Let's get a move on."

The next morning, Dougan turned in his list to Sandy: Beans, rice, potatoes, flour, lard, bacon, eggs, coffee, baking powder, salt, pepper, onions, canned tomatoes, canned milk and canned fruit. There were some unusual items that Sandy wondered about: Garlic, canned fruit, canned salmon, cooking wine, and some spices he had never heard of. Sandy took the list to Tommy Larson. He also ordered a keg of assorted horseshoes and several pounds of horseshoe nails.

Billy needed 16 horse blankets, seven riding saddles, nine pack saddles and 18 pack boxes or panniers. He would have to borrow from Grandpa W.D. and Uncle Kyle. He also had to get the fishing gear ready. Dad had a fly rod and he had the one he got for his 9th birthday and first pack trip. Hopefully, Grandpa and Uncle Kyle would remember theirs. Ralph needed one, too. Billy found four large tarps that would work for tents, ground cloths or even blankets. Behind the ice house, he found the fire grate, tongs, and tripod. All the camping cookware was in the house back porch. He counted out eight tin plates, cups, buckets, fry pans and the Dutch oven, coffee pot and enough silverware. Getting ready seemed like a lot of work. "I hope it's worth it," he said to himself.

Sandy asked Richard Johnson to help with the horseshoeing. Richard started out as a farrier before he got his own ranch. They decided to work inside the barn where it was cool and controlled with fewer distractions for the horse.

It was a pretty sight to see the whole herd of horses splashing across the creek and kicking up the dust as they galloped toward the corral. Richard and Sandy swung their lassos above their heads as they rounded up the herd. Billy was there to close the big gate. Once in the corral, the horses settled down and ate some oats spread in the feeder troughs. The pecking order still applied as Cindy and Wolf laid their ears back and demanded to eat first. Some of the horses were used to the drill and they were shod first. Billy watched carefully.

"Do you want to do the next one?" asked Richard.

"Can I do Pedro?"

"We've never shod him before. No telling what he might do," replied Sandy. "Maybe you should try old Judy first."

Richard and Sandy worked most of the morning and each did three horses. They first haltered the horse and tied him to a high ring in the box stall. Carefully and gently, they would rub down the back and shoulder of the animal, down the leg to the hock. Then, they would lift the leg and foot on to their laps. They wore leather aprons. The next step was to clean out the hoof and frog (the recess behind the hoof rim), float the hoof level with a long coarse rasp and then pick a new horseshoe from the barrel that would fit. The shoes came in several sizes with the usual bend and eight holes around the rim. Sometimes they couldn't find a shoe that fit, so the shoe had to be customized. The iron shoe was heated red hot in the forge and then shaped with tongs, anvil and hammer to fit exactly. Sandy had outfitted the blacksmith shop with a small forge, and all the necessary tools. Billy got the job of cranking the blower for the forge.

When the hoof was level and clean, the shoe was laid on and a nail was driven through the shoe, into the hoof and through. The sharp exposed point was crimped over and then a second nail was driven through. Finally, all eight nails were through. The shod hoof was then placed on the floor and the nails were seated, clinched tightly and the protruding ends cut off. Then, the hoof was lifted up again and the hoof edges rasped flush with the edge of the shoe.

Billy remembered the "For Want of a Nail" verse mom

used to tell him whenever he felt like he was too little or unimportant:

For want of a nail the shoe was lost.
For want of a shoe the horse was lost.
For want of a horse the rider was lost.
For want of a rider the battle was lost.
For want of a battle the kingdom was lost.
And all for the want of a horseshoe nail.

It was hard work, stooping over and holding up the hoof while holding the shoe and driving the nails. Some of the horses added weight by leaning on you. Some of the horses wouldn't hold still and some of the horses freaked out. The hind legs were harder. The farrier stood at the flank of the horse. He gently slid his hand down the leg to the hock, raised and extended the leg behind the horse. When the leg was fully extended, the powerful leg muscles were not as strong to bring the leg down and forward. A good farrier could shoe a horse in one hour.

It was Billy's turn to try Judy. Judy was patient and quiet, but she was a leaner. Richard and Sandy watched and handed Billy the tools. Cleaning and floating the hoof was easiest. Attaching the shoe was harder. Billy finally got the knack of holding the hoof and loose shoe with one hand while balancing the leg on his lap and starting to drive the nails with the other hand. "This is harder than it looks," sighed Billy as the sweat formed on his brow.

"Be careful of that sharp protruding nail end, Billy," cautioned Richard. "Bend it over as soon as you get it through."

Richard had no sooner said that when Judy straightened out her leg and drove the nail into Billy's thigh, right through the leather apron. Billy dropped the hammer and rolled on the floor. He yelled the "D" word. He was hurt, embarrassed and bleeding. He was trying hard not to cry.

Sandy looked at the puncture. He squeezed out some more blood. "It looks clean and shallow; it will be okay. You up to finishing the job, son?"

"I'd like to try. I'm sorry I said a bad word," gulped Billy.

The shoe was dangling from Judy's foot. Judy seemed nonplussed by the commotion. Billy started over. He snugged up the first nail and quickly bent it over; then, the second and third. Finally, all eight nails were in and clinched. Billy gasped for breath. "I think I'll do something else for a living."

Richard and Sandy laughed. "You're ready for Pedro now?"

Billy had been training Pedro to lift his foot all summer. He also had been getting him used to having a hand on his flank. Billy had removed rocks stuck in the frog of Pedro's hoof and he thought he could do at least the front feet now.

"We can do this together, old boy," he said as he rubbed down Pedro and grabbed the hock. Pedro stood quivering and tense as Billy floated the hoof. Pedro had an extra long hoof nail on the left foot, so the extra needed to be nipped off before the shoe was fitted. The hoof clipping formed a crescent. Billy considered keeping it as his remembrance of shoeing Pedro for the first time. He could put it in his collection which included a rattlesnake rattle, several arrowheads and a coyote skull. Now, it was time to nail the shoe to the hoof. He felt Pedro shudder as he tapped the nail home, but Pedro held still. The young cowboy clinched the nail and drove in the rest. The shoe was level and square. Billy smoothed out the edge with the rasp.

"Good job, Billy; now do the other hoof," praised Richard.

"I think you better do the hind feet," said Billy.

Billy did the other front and Richard started on the back. He lifted and extended the left leg. Pedro tried to bring the leg forward, but at full extension, there wasn't much power. Billy rubbed Pedro's neck and jaw as he talked gently and reassuringly. "Easy old boy, everything's going to be all right."

Richard floated and sized the hoof. The number 3 shoe

just fit. He had two nails in when Pedro stretched his leg out far enough to catch the swinging stall gate with the partially attached shoe. He then brought the leg forward swinging the gate into Richard, smacking his cheek and ear with the gate frame. Richard went sprawling under Pedro. Pedro stepped backward and stood on Richard's hand with this newly shod hoof. Billy did his best to calm Pedro as Richard crawled out from between the horse's legs.

"Are you okay?" Billy urgently called.

"I've never had that happen before," admitted Richard. "I guess I'm okay. I feel like I've been in the ring with Jack Dempsey."

Sandy came running in. "I heard a big bang. What happened? Are you okay?"

Richard's cheek and ear were beginning to swell. He held his hand up to his chest. "You're going to have to finish Pedro," he said to Sandy and Billy. "I'm going to take a break."

Billy ran to the ice house and got a big chunk of ice and a towel. They made a pack for Richard's cheek and hand.

"I hope your hand isn't broken," said Sandy as he wrapped the towel and ice around the hand. There was a crescent shaped bruise forming across the back of the hand but everything seemed aligned. "Can you move your fingers?"

Richard slowly moved all the fingers of his bruised left hand. "Just keep it iced for now. We might have to get you in to see Doc Bateman," said Sandy. "Billy, let's finish Pedro."

Pedro seemed to sense the urgency of the situation and handled the shoeing like an old pro. Billy tapped in the nails while Sandy held the leg and foot.

"That's 12 done — four to go!" yelled Billy.

That evening, they recounted the shoeing adventures and the day's events. Richard Johnson was bruised, but not broken. The summer fallow team had only two more strips to do and the last of the hay was stacked. All that was left to do to get ready was to shoe the last four horses, organize the packs and groceries and get everybody's personal gear together.

"We've still got to shoe Paint and Rascal," Billy reminded them. "Will Richard be able to help?"

Dougan volunteered to help. "I've seen a horse thrown before and I think we can do it."

Sandy had done it before too, but throwing a horse wasn't easy for a cowboy and could be dangerous for the horse.

The next morning, the whole crew was on the corral rail for the horse throw. Billy led Rascal to the snubbing pole. Sandy looped a long rope over Rascal's head and then behind both hind legs. They tightened the rope pulling his legs under him. Then, as Rascal struggled, the rope was tightened and another rope around the front legs was tightened. As Rascal fell over, Billy released the snubbing rope. The feet were trussed so Rascal couldn't kick free. The horse that lived up to his name lay in the middle of the corral terrified, quivering and snorting.

"Billy, why don't you ride over to Grandpa's and get the two horses for Uncle Kyle and Grandpa? Dougan and I can finish up here," Sandy called. "Maybe Grandma will feed you lunch."

Billy was always ready to ride to Spring Hill, although shoeing horses was pretty exciting, too. Pedro's new shoes clicked on the rocks as he rode the trail. He inspected the fence and gates as he rode across the west pasture. The cattle were spread out and contented. He could see several bulls paired up with cows. They weren't fighting each other, which meant there was plenty of breeding for them all to do. In one month, there would be more competition.

He was lost in thought about the mountain trip when Pedro reared up at a buzzing rattlesnake in the middle of the trail. Billy quickly grabbed the horn as Pedro's newly shod hoof came crashing down on the snake. Pedro stomped the snake a few more times as it writhed on the trail. Billy dismounted and found a stick to move the snake. He then stood on its head as he cut off the rattle with his pocket knife.

"Good job, Pedro," he praised his horse. "You and I make a great team. Maybe we'll be in the movies like Hoot Gibson."

He got to Spring Hill about 11:00 A.M. He said hello to Grandma and went out to find Grandpa. Grandpa had the horses saddled and in the corral.

"Howdy, Billy, you all ready for the pack trip?" greeted Grandpa.

"I can't wait to go!" exclaimed Billy. "We got all the horses shod and nobody died. I got to shoe the fronts of Judy and Pedro, too. And Pedro killed a rattlesnake!"

Grandpa shared in Billy's enthusiasm. "If I'd known you were a farrier, I would have hired you to shoe these two horses. You're just like your dad when he was your age," added Grandpa.

"Tell me about dad, Grandpa. You started on our last ride, but we ran out of time," begged Billy.

"Your dad liked to do things; explore, get into mischief in contrast to his older brother Kyle. Kyle liked to study about things. Sandy liked the outdoors, hunting and fishing, riding horseback and sicking the dog on the cat. He was smart enough, but never did well in school. I guess he was too interested in figuring out how things worked rather than studying about them," Grandpa said with a chuckle. "Is that why he knows so much about ranching and machinery and everything?" asked Billy.

"That's a good part of it, Billy, but he eventually did get some book learning. When he was 16 and thought he knew everything, I sent him off to military academy in Missouri. I hoped he would learn to study, take orders, and behave himself," said Grandpa.

"Did he get into trouble?" Billy questioned.

"Well, let's just say he was a little rebellious. He didn't

want to go to school anymore and even talked about leaving Montana," Grandpa recounted.

"What happened? He isn't like that now," observed Billy.

"I think he found out that he had it pretty good here on the ranch and that he really wanted to come back and be a rancher."

"But how about his studies?" said Billy.

"The academy caught him up fast and he became a good student. He studied all he could about farming and ranching. I think he was out to prove to himself and me that he could be better than I."

"So you're in competition?" asked Billy.

"Not from my side of it, but your dad is focused on being the best and biggest rancher around. He even has eyes on my political career," laughed Grandpa.

"Did he ever want to be a banker like you?"

"No, Kyle was always playing banker while Sandy was hunting coyotes. Kyle went to the University of Montana and majored in finance. He never wanted to be a rancher. Your dad never wanted to be a banker. At least the brothers didn't have to compete," Grandpa joked.

"It's time for noon dinner," called Grandma Lilly.

They came in and washed up. Eating at Grandma Lilly's was always a treat. Billy told Grandma about the rattlesnake, shoeing the horses and Burt's riding horseback.

"I'm sure you men will have a good time," commented Lilly, "I'm not so sure about Burt. Why is she going?"

"Just to see the mountains and get away," answered Billy.

Billy led the two saddle horses to the gate and climbed on Pedro. "I'll see you at the trailhead in a couple of days. Take good care of my sisters while we're gone," he called as he waved his hat and headed for the T-6.

Part II

Chapter X

"Wake up, Billy. It's daylight and your day one on the mountain pack trip," Burt cheerfully called.

Billy bounded out of bed and downstairs. His boots were by the back door and his hat on the porch. He ran to the barn where Dougan and Dad were laying out the pack boxes, saddles, cooking equipment, food, lanterns, axes, fencing supplies and fishing gear. The items were stacked on 6 x 6 foot square tarpaulins, then wrapped like a Christmas present in the tarp and tied tightly with a rope. There were 18 packages sitting around the barnyard.

"Good morning, cowboy," called Dad as he cinched up a pack box. We're trying to get the weight distributed so the boxes are about 100 pounds each. Is breakfast ready yet?"

"Not quite," replied Billy. "What can I do?"

"Bring over a couple of pack animals. Ben and Cindy should be first," said Dad.

They put the heavy horse blankets on the pair and then the pack saddles. Each pack saddle was a frame that fit over the horse's back like a cap and cinched down. The frame was well padded and fitted with rings and hooks for the boxes or panniers. The tarp-wrapped boxes or bundles were tied securely to the saddles. Finally, a large folded tarp was placed over the entire load and cinched down with a diamond hitch.

"Dad, will you teach me how to tie a diamond hitch on this trip?" asked Billy.

"You betcha, cowboy," replied Dad. "We'll make you a first class packer and wrangler before the trip is over."

They heaved and tugged and got all nine pack animals loaded by 7:30 A.M. They were lined up along the corral rail switching their tails and pawing the dirt.

"Let's go have breakfast," Dougan suggested. "We've got a lot of riding to do before dark."

As they ate big bowls of oatmeal, homemade toast and jam, eggs and milk, they planned the next two days. Billy and Dougan would take the horses and packs to the trail head. Burt, Sandy, W.D., Kyle and Ralph Burton would ride in the car and join up at the trail head tomorrow morning. They would start out by mid morning and try to get over Blackleaf Pass to the North Fork of the Teton river and camp the first day, then plan a day at a time until they got to Big River Meadows.

The anticipation was electric as they saddled the riding horses and roped up the pack trains. There were two strings of eight each. Billy atop Pedro led one, Dougan on Wolf led the other. Burt, Betty, Beryl, Sandy and the haying crew all cheered and waved as the trains went through the big corral gate and onto the Blackleaf trail at 8:00 A.M.

"We'll see you at the canyon tomorrow morning!" yelled Sandy. "Be careful!"

"Watch out for bears and Indians," yelled Beryl.

"We've got to set a fast pace to cover the 20 miles by supper time," stated Billy. "I know the trail. I'll lead."

The trail led out of the wide U-shaped coulee onto the flat, gravelly bench, both remnants of the ancient glacier that carved the front land. The rocky bench was covered with the limestone glacial until that made it all seem like a gravel road. Billy could see the fossil shapes of shells and coral in the rocks. It was good the horses were shod as 20 miles of this stuff would have worn down their hooves to the quick.

They went through the line fences of the Fields' ranch and then the Olson's. They were careful to close all the gates, first to keep any livestock from escaping and closing all escape routes in case any of the horses broke free and headed for home.

They crossed into the burn zone from the prairie wildfire. The naked ground looked like a moonscape. Badger and gopher holes were exposed. There were so many it was hard to believe that any grass had grown between them. The horses kicked up sooty dust as they crossed the scarred hills. There was no sign of life except the horses.

"We better get to water pretty soon. This black desert reminds me of hell," said Dougan as he coughed and snorted in the black dust.

"Olson's stock reservoir is over the next hill. I'll bet the horses can smell it," said Billy.

They dismounted and allowed all the horses to drink. There was no shade there and the flies were bothering the horses and riders. "Let's go another mile to Blackleaf Creek for lunch. There's a good place to get some shade and the horses can do a little grazing," said Billy.

Blackleaf Creek meandered down a wide coulee after

coming out of Blackleaf Canyon. There were clumps of aspen and cottonwoods as well as thick brushy willows along its banks. Numerous beaver dams and ponds created a riparian retreat for wildlife. As they came near the creek, several white-tails bounded out of the brush. They heard the slap of a beaver tail across the pond and watched a flight of ducks lift off the water.

"This is a good place for a break," Billy called to Dougan.

They ground tethered the horses and sat down at the creek bank. Mom had packed a lunch of ham and cheese sandwiches, pickles and gingersnaps. They watched a few trout rising in the beaver pond, then ate with great relish.

"I'd like to toss a fly at those brookies, but I guess we don't have time," Billy said wistfully.

"Trout would taste good for supper tonight," Dougan replied, "but I'm afraid the fishing tackle is at the bottom of the packs."

"The horses have had enough rest and grazing to get us the rest of the way. We better get started if we want to make camp before dark," reasoned Billy.

They started to gather up the horses and re-form the string when all the horses went on alert. There was a commotion in the brush near the creek. They could hear the grunting and then they saw the grizzly. He was as big as Dad's bull. They were downwind and about 50 yards from him. Billy got a whiff of the bear's musty aroma. The terrified horses were straining at their ropes.

"Just ease them all back slowly," whispered Dougan. "He doesn't seem to be ready to attack."

They mounted the horses and slowly the two pack strings walked out of the creek bottom. The bear was still watching as they reached the hill top.

"That's a big grizzly," said Billy. "There must be a lot of things for him to eat down by the creek."

"I'm glad it wasn't us," Dougan whistled.

Billy surveyed the creek bottom and meadows with the mountains rearing up only a few miles away now. "This is a real pretty spot. It would be a great spot for a ranch. Great pasture, hay land, water, winter shelter and good fishing, too. Some day, I'll have a ranch in a place like this," dreamed Billy.

They followed the gravelly ridge westward. The mountains loomed higher with each mile. The flora began to change from grass to scattered scrub pines. The open range horses were skittish as they went past the scrub looking for bears behind every clump. Flatland horses were always extra nervous in the mountains; if they had a chance, they would bolt for the open spaces.

As they approached the 1000-foot stone wall that jutted out of the prairie, Dougan wondered just how they were going to make it through. Blackleaf Creek seemed to come out of the rock. Now, taller pines and spruce softened the cliff base and aspen clumps the creek bottoms. They felt it before they saw the narrow slot in the wall. Wind poured through the gorge and hit them in the face. Blackleaf Creek had cut through the cliff face. The gap was just wide enough for the creek and the two skid tracks.

Billy told Dougan, "They say the highest winds ever measured come down this gorge. It is impossible to stand or walk against it. It's a good thing it's calmer today."

They marveled at the strata exposed on the cliff face. Way at the bottom, there were trees and logs, higher up, shells and coral, mud-shale layers and colors of grey-black, white and tan.

"We can see all the geologic history in one place," commented Dougan. "This is fascinating."

"And see that vertical slot?" pointed Billy, "That's the opening to Volcano Reef. When the atmosphere is right, a tornado forms at the top of the slot and it looks like the cliff face is erupting."

They proceeded up the horn of the canyon to a gate across the gorge. "That gate will keep the horses from escaping back to the T-6," said Billy. "We'll close it behind us. It's there for the cattle that are up here grazing on summer permits. I think the Parkers and Knowltons hold the leases."

The canyon opened into a circular basin. There was timber along the creek and on the south slope. The North Slope was grassy with numerous dead tree spars and fallen logs from the 1910 fire.

"We built our house out of logs like those," said Billy. "My Dad skidded them all the way to our ranch. We followed the skid ruts on our way here."

There was a small log cabin at the site, a hut for the cattle tenders. "This is where we can camp," said Billy. "We can put the grub in the cabin as its bear proof." They unloaded all the packs, took the saddles off the horses and turned the horses out to graze. They put hobbles on Wolf and Zig, the leaders of the herd. They also tied horse bells on several horses, too. By that time, it was 9:00 P.M.

"I'm famished," said Billy. "What do we have to eat?"

Dougan ordered, "Gather some wood, start a fire and put some water on to boil while I rustle up some grub. We don't have time for any fancy cooking, so we'll eat out of a can tonight."

They filled up on canned beans and bread with canned peaches for dessert. Billy drank kid coffee and Dougan the regular stuff. They sat by the fire and listened to the horse bells as the stars came out.

Dougan remarked, "This is as fine a supper and atmosphere as I've had anywhere."

"Where have you had the next best?" asked Billy.

"There's a hotel in Chicago where they serve steaks so juicy, thick and tender you can cut them with a butter knife. The waiters stand around and fill your glasses and put your napkin on your lap. They would even cut up your meat if you asked them. They play soft music and offer you big cigars. It's pretty fancy," said Dougan. "Or, there's this place in Paris where they served five different courses, each with its own plate. They started with soup, then fish, then meat and vegetables, then salad, and finally dessert."

Billy was impressed. "I want to go someplace fancy like that. How did you get to go?"

"Oh, I've been around and done a lot of things."

"Where did you learn to cook?" asked Billy.

"To tell the truth, I've never really been a chef, but I've worked in a lot of kitchens and it kind of rubbed off. I cooked some in the army and once in a big institution back east," offered Dougan.

"Like a college or something?" asked Billy.

"Something like that," answered Dougan.

They flopped out their bedrolls on a grassy spot and slept under the stars. Billy was so tired he didn't even feel the roots and rocks.

Chapter XI

It was early dawn when Dougan called to Billy. "Do you hear the horse bells?" There was silence. Billy got up quickly and pulled on his boots. He could see Wolf still hobbled, but Zig was no where to be seen. No other horses were visible, either.

He caught Wolf and saddled up. "I'll see if I can find them," he called to Dougan. "You can fix breakfast."

Billy rode to the top of a ridge and looked in all directions. He called to Pedro. No sounds. He saw a few cows and two elk higher up on the ridge. He could see back to the canyon gate and they weren't there. He turned back and saw Pedro trotting toward him. "I knew you'd come. Now, show me where the rest of the herd is hiding," Billy said proudly.

Pedro led off to the south and through some rather dense timber. In the clearing beyond, Billy saw the herd. Punch was dancing and pulling on something at the edge of the clearing. When he got there, he found her tangled in some wire and abandoned logging machinery. He didn't have any wire cutters with him, but he managed to bend and break the wire strands. Punch bounded free but she had some cuts on her shoulders and front feet.

Billy caught several horses by their halters and roped them together. They started back to camp and all the horses followed. Half way back, he found the hobbles that old Zig had slipped. Punch followed limping a little, but the bleeding had stopped.

Dougan saw them coming and walked out to lead a few more to the tie up rail. "I was afraid we'd have to walk home carrying all those packs."

They secured all the horses and then had breakfast. Dougan had made hot cakes, eggs, bacon and coffee. He made enough hot cakes so they could have cold bacon-hot cake sandwiches on the trail.

After cleaning up, they started saddling the horses.

"At least we don't have to re-pack much," said Billy. "Next camp, everything will be out."

"I don't expect them until about 11," said Dougan. "They have to pack their personal stuff, load up the girls and their stuff for two weeks and drive to Spring Hill, and then pick up W.D. and Kyle before they start."

"And then they have to drive across all that gravel to get here. I hope they don't have a flat tire or a breakdown," added Billy.

It was just 11:00 when the car came bouncing over the rocky road. The entourage tumbled out and stretched. "I only hit my head on the roof of the car three times; good thing we didn't have an open top or I'd be back there in the middle of the road," joked Burt.

"Just getting you ready to ride old Paint," teased Sandy.

W.D. was wearing his revolver and Sandy had his 30-30 saddle carbine. They also brought Billy's .22. "No telling when we might need these; there may be bears, outlaws or a wild Indian up here in the mountains," Grandpa said with a wink at Billy.

Billy told Dad about Punch. They went over to examine her. "It's mostly an abrasion and not too deep," said Sandy as he picked up the foot and brushed away the dried blood and debris. "We'll have to give her a lighter load today. Billy, would you ride Punch and I'll ride Pedro?"

Billy reluctantly agreed. He remembered being bucked off Punch last spring and how could he not ride Pedro? Billy weighed about 110 pounds and Sandy 180, so it was a reasonable request.

"Just for today though, Dad," Billy added.

Everybody brought their personal gear and packed it into saddle bags or tied it to the back of the saddle with the latigo straps. Burt had a big bag of stuff. "I don't think we can get all that in," teased Sandy. "You'd think we were going to Chicago."

"Just because you wear the same clothes for two weeks and smell like and old bear doesn't mean I have to!" snapped Burt.

They parked the car at the trailhead and made sure there was no food or other scent to attract bears. The pack strings were roped together and the seven riders and nine pack animals headed up the trail. Dougan led one string of five and Sandy the other. Billy, Grandpa, Kyle, Burt and Ralph Burton led the procession.

W.D. pointed ahead toward a far ridgeline. "That's Blackleaf Pass and you can see the trail crossing that slide."

"How far and how high, Grandpa?" asked Billy.

"I think it's about six miles and 7000 feet, to answer your two questions," Grandpa replied. "We should be there by 4:00 P.M. It's only a short downhill from there to camp."

The trail stayed near the creek. They could hear the roar of Blackleaf Falls ahead.

"That's the falls that my sister Beryl fell over when she was six years old," Billy told Ralph Burton. "The family was up here on a picnic and Beryl fell in the creek above the falls. We all watched helplessly as she was swept downstream and over the edge."

"I guess she lived," said Ralph.

"We all thought she was dead. We looked over the edge into the pool below and she was lying face down in the water," said Billy.

"What happened then?" asked Ralph urgently.

"My Dad jumped off the cliff into a tall tree that was growing near the pool. He slid down the tree and grabbed Beryl from the water. He pounded her on the back and she woke up!" exclaimed Billy.

"That fall must have been 50 feet," guessed Ralph. "She was lucky."

"Lucky or blessed," said Billy. "My Dad doesn't believe in luck. He says everything happens for a reason."

The trail switch backed up to the top of the falls and continued along the creek. Finally, they stopped at a small pond in a small cirque. "This is the start of Blackleaf Creek," said Grandpa. "A spring forms this pond fed by those snow banks and glaciers high up on Mt. Frazier."

"This is the best tasting water on earth," said Billy as he lay on his stomach and drank from the pool.

"What's this stuff?" said Ralph as he plucked some white fuzz from the bushes.

"It's mountain goat wool," replied Grandpa. The goats come here to water and rub their wool off on the bushes. The Indians used to collect it to make liners for their garments or for decorations on their clothes and headdresses."

"Look up there," pointed Billy. "There are goats way up on that ledge above us."

Mt. Frazier towered above them. High steep cliffs dissolved into slopes of talus that came all the way down to the spring. Above the cliffs, snow filled the crevices and north facing slopes and a glacier filled a cirque near the top.

"Frazier is nearly 9000 feet tall. It's the main mountain we see from the ranch" said Sandy who had joined the group.

"Mom, how are you doing?" asked Billy.

"So far, so good," replied Burt. "I hope I can get back on Judy."

"Have you tasted this water, Aunt Minerva? It's better than

lemonade," said Ralph, "Just lie on this flat rock and drink like the horses."

Burt got down on her knees and leaned over into the pool. It was so clear that she put her whole face into the water without realizing it.

"You're right, Ralph. It's cold and refreshing."

"This is the last water before the long ascent to Blackleaf Pass," said Sandy. "Drink your fill and let the horses drink. We might as well eat now, too."

Billy and Dougan had pancake and bacon sandwiches. The group that came in the car had ham and cheese sandwiches, cookies and a Hershey bar. Billy traded sandwiches with Ralph and begged for a bite of candy bar.

Sandy and Dougan started up the grade trailing the pack strings.

"We'll try to push straight through to camp. The rest of you can poke along," Sandy called back over his shoulder.

"Goodbye, Pedro," Billy yelled back.

They watched as the pack strings climbed the switchbacks through the rockslide above them. Soon, the horses looked like ants climbing up a wall.

"Do we have to go up there?" asked Burt. "It goes straight up. What if the horse steps off the edge?"

"Don't worry, Mom. The horse knows where his feet are," reassured Billy.

The five riders were watered, fed and rested. They started up the trail with Grandpa leading, Billy trailing, and Kyle, Ralph and Burt in the middle. The trail was covered with loose sharp rocks and was bordered by big rocks that had been pushed aside by the forest service trail crews. Looking across the huge rockslide, Billy saw marmots and pica scurrying for cover and heard their whistles of warning.

"Don't look down, Mom. Look at those wild flowers growing between the rocks," Billy yelled ahead.

The first switchback turned sharply and the trail was almost above the trailing riders. Small rocks bounced down from the upper trail. Billy looked up at Grandpa as he passed.

Grandpa called down to Billy. "You might have to get off and lead Punch over those sharp rocks so she doesn't re-injure that foot."

"I'll watch her closely, Grandpa," Billy returned.

They climbed steadily up the slope and then the trail traversed a long, open slide. The only vegetation was some tiny shrubs and mosses that could survive the high altitude, harsh winds and deep snow in the winter. Brilliant patches of bright pink creeping phlox dotted the slope. Soft fuzzy pink pussy toes grew in the gravel, their texture belying their hardiness. They could see the pass ahead. A snow bank filled the north slope of the notch. Burt noticed some avalanche lilies at the edge of the receding snow. When they all reached the top, they looked over the divide to a wide green valley. A brisk wind blew through the gap.

"What a beautiful and harsh place," exclaimed Burt.

"I hope it was worth the trip," said W.D.

"What do you mean by that?" retorted Burt.

"I'm still wondering just why you came, Burt."

"Just to check up on you and your boys," she said with a sly smile.

The procession started the descent into the Teton canyon. The trail hugged the cliff face and was sometimes so narrow that you could reach out and touch the mountain as you rode by. Billy dismounted and led Punch down. The horses were sliding and skidding as they applied their brakes going down. The riders were thrown to the front of the saddles or were riding the horn.

Burt felt herself sexually stimulated with the sway and bounce of the descent. At first, she felt ashamed or guilty and stood up in the saddle, but her knees started hurting. She finally relaxed and accepted it as a perk on this harrowing descent.

After coming down about 1000 feet, the vegetation of the lower valley started to appear. First, came the grasses, stunted willow and aspens; then, the alpine fir and finally the taller fir and spruce. The trail became soft and slightly muddy. The scent of the forest filled the air. Burt was flooded with thoughts of the men in her life. She wondered if they felt romantic in the mountain splendor. What was it that they got out of roughing it in the wilderness?

She first thought of Sandy: Dependable, predictable, driven to impress his father, reverent, quiet, innovative but not very romantic. She was ten years older than Sandy. Did he ever wish for a younger woman now that she was 45? They hadn't made love since the spring work started. They had talked of more children, but at age 45 it might not be possible. She was uncertain if he really wanted more children, especially another girl. She yearned for more intimacy. Was she responsible for the recent coolness?

Then, Billy. He was already exhibiting his father's traits. He was a little more studious than Sandy was at his age. He idolized this father and wanted to follow in his father's footsteps — even to attending military academy. She wished he shared her love of literature and poetry, but she was so proud of him as she watched him become a man.

Then, there was W.D. She had always felt some tension with him. He probably thought she married Sandy for his money. He was always cool toward her when ranch or financial subjects were discussed. It seemed that he felt she was intruding on the men's mountain trip. W.D. was used to getting his way. He was powerful and influential in the county and state. He had led sheriff posses and participated in the vigilante hangings of horse thieves. He was not one to cross.

And what about that mysterious stranger, Jack Dougan?

She hadn't had feelings like she had around him since she was a schoolgirl back in Iowa. She was flattered that she was still attractive to a younger man. Was he just playing up to her or did he really like and admire her? He didn't talk much about the ten years between the war and now. Obviously, he had a lot of experiences and travel. Was he a fugitive? Did he have a family? What was his education? What was she thinking? This fantasy was a recipe for heartache, loss and disaster. Was anything worth that?

She was stirred from her thoughts by the sound of rushing water.

"Mom, this is Teton River. We have to ford here," yelled Billy over the sounds of the river. "You might get your feet wet."

The horses went single file through the swiftly flowing stream. The water came up to the horses bellies. "Hold your legs out or you'll get your feet wet," called Billy.

When they got to the far side, all the horses drank their fill.

"We're just about to camp where there is a good spring for drinking, but you can drink here with the horses if you want to," said W.D.

They heard the whinnying of horses ahead and soon the herd was reunited.

The camp was situated at the junction of the Teton River and Boulder Creek. A gravel bar spread out along the bank and several large ponderosa pines shaded the park-like area. Further back in the forest, long poles had been secured to the trees and the horses were all tied along the rails. Sandy and Dougan had unloaded all the packs and were busy setting up camp.

"It's about time you slowpokes got here," Dougan said.

"We're just in time for dinner. Why haven't you got it ready yet?" said Grandpa.

Burt yelled, "I don't think I can get off this horse I'm so stiff."

Sandy came over and helped her off. She gave him a little peck on the cheek as she slid past him to the ground. He helped her walk out the kinks.

"This might be the best meal of the trip," commented Dougan. "We've got fresh meat only one day out. After today, it's all canned, dried or smoked."

They dined high that evening on grilled steak and potatoes baked in the Dutch oven.

"You boys better get busy and provide for the table," said Dougan. "Catch a few trout or bring me a rabbit or a couple of grouse; otherwise, we might starve."

"Trout for breakfast," yelled Billy and Ralph as they set out to find the fishing gear.

"Don't go too far, boys. It'll be dark in only a couple of hours and you still need to make up your bed rolls," cautioned Sandy.

We'll keep the horses tied up tonight," said Sandy. "There is no line fence or natural barrier to hold them. Tomorrow will be a shorter day with good grazing at the next camp."

The five adults did the dishes and then hung the food high up on a rope suspended between two trees.

"I saw some bear sign on the trail across the river, so they're around," said W.D. "Nothing like a slab of pork belly to draw them."

It was a cloudless evening. They unrolled their beds on a grassy flat and then sat around the fire to watch the stars come out. They were startled by crashing in the brush behind them, but it was only Billy and Ralph coming back.

"We caught some fish!" exclaimed Ralph as the held up a string of small fish.

"I could eat all of those in one bite," teased Grandpa.

"Make a holding pen at the river's edge to keep them cold," said Dougan. "Of course, clean them first."

The boys made a rock rimmed pod at the river bank and placed the string of fish there. They then laid out their bed rolls.

"It's been a long day and time to turn in," said Sandy. "I've got us a good spot behind those fir trees, Burt."

"I'm stiff everywhere," said Burt. "My shoulders and back are as achy as my butt and knees."

Sandy massaged her shoulders. "You need to learn to relax your upper body as you ride."

She leaned back into him. "Make love to me tonight," she whispered.

Sandy stammered, "Out here in camp? Everybody will hear us. Besides, I don't have my skin."

"We can be quiet and don't worry about pregnancy. We can name him River."

Chapter XII: Boulder Creek

Everybody was up at dawn. The first night on the trail, nobody sleeps. The rocks and roots are still too hard. The sounds are too loud. The stars are too bright. By the second or third night, the rocks and roots get softer. The fire was crackling and the coffee pot was boiling. Dougan was mixing up biscuits while Sandy, Grandpa and Kyle were checking on the horses.

"Hey, Billy," Dougan called. "Bring those fish up for breakfast."

Billy and Ralph went to the river. The fish were gone! They could see where the string tether had been pulled out.

"Something got our fish!" cried Billy. "It could've been a mink, a wolverine or a bear."

Then they saw the large bear track in the mud.

"That track is a foot long!" exclaimed Billy. "That bear had to come right through camp to get those fish. I'm glad he was hungry for fish and not me."

They walked back to the cook fire, disappointed but excited to tell the story.

"You'll just have to catch some more" said Mom with enthusiasm.

Breakfast was delicious; bacon, eggs, biscuits and grape nuts with hot water and canned milk.

"You must have been a cook in the army," said Sandy. "This is fighting food."

They packed up camp, loaded the horses and were ready to hit the trail.

"Dad, can I have Pedro back? Punch is doing better," asked Billy.

"I think that will be okay," said Sandy. "Today's ride is shorter and the trail is mostly in the forest."

"And Dad, can Ralph and I stay here and fish for a while and then come up to camp?"

"That will be okay, son, but be in camp by 3:00 o'clock. Do you have your pocket watch?"

Billy had his watch and checked the time. They tied up the two horses and went fishing.

The pack string and riders forded Boulder Creek and headed up the trail toward Crazy Creek Pass. Boulder Creek originated in a glacial cirque or "hanging valley" about six miles up the trail. They would camp there for two nights and give the horses two days of grazing and everybody a rest and opportunity to explore the high mountain meadow.

The first three miles was through dense old timber. It was quiet, dark and musty in the woods. Years of windfalls and light starved undergrowth had left mounds of debris.

"If a fire got started here, it would burn for a season," said W.D. "The Indians used to start fires on purpose to clean out the forest and produce more food for the game."

"I would be terrified if a forest fire started here. We would be trapped," said Burt as she surveyed the dense forest.

They came to a windfall lying across the trail. It was a rather old log about 18 inches in diameter. They tried to skirt it, but the surrounding forest was too dense.

"We'll have to cut a section out" said Sandy. "I wish we had the crosscut saw, but at least the axes are sharp."

Dougan and Sandy chopped out the section of the log blocking the trail. They heaved and pried the section out of the way and resumed the ride. After another 30 minutes, they broke out into open meadow and a boggy trail. The horse's feet sucked as they stepped through the bog.

"I hope this is not quicksand!" exclaimed Burt.

"Just lie flat or stand on the horse as he goes under," teased Dougan. "There's got to be a bottom down there somewhere."

"You must think I've just got off the turnip truck" returned Burt.

"Gullible but gorgeous," quipped Dougan as he tipped his hat.

"Let's take a break," broke in Sandy. "There's a nice spring up and just across this bog before we climb up to Boulder Creek Cirque."

The Teton River was fast and cold. There were numerous large boulders in the stream to create good cover for trout. Billy tied on Dad's favorite fly, the royal coachman. Billy had been practicing fly casting ever since his first "Big River" trip when he was nine. He was getting pretty good. Ralph Burton didn't know much about fly fishing, but he wanted to learn. He had fished with worms, but there weren't any worms to be found up here in the mountains.

Billy waded into the icy cold water and started to pay out his line. He explained to Ralph the position and the rhythm back and forth. "Ten o'clock to 2 o'clock, strip out the line and wait until the back cast loop has formed behind you. Let the pole do the work. Then, bring it forward and point the pole to where you want the fly. Let go of the slack loop in your left hand and the fly should settle on the water."

Ralph watched the swooping line form giant loops and then straighten out depositing the fly at the top of the riffle. The fly barely hit the water when a nice 12-inch cutthroat smacked the fly. The fish raced around the pool, upstream and down.

Ralph yelled, "Don't lose him; I can taste him already!"

Billy backed up the bank and beached the fish. "It's a beauty," he beamed. "Ralph, could you cut a willow branch for a stringer while I go after his brother?"

Billy caught three more in that pool before handing the rod to Ralph. "It's your turn, Ralph. I'll stand beside you and help."

Ralph tried to remember all the positions, the timing and the delivery. He started his back cast and then started forward. Snap went the line behind him. "That was like cracking a whip," he said.

"We better look at the fly," said Billy. "Sometimes you can snap off the fly with a whip crack." Sure enough, the fly was gone. "Good thing we have some extras," he said as he tied on another royal coachman.

Ralph was a little better with his next attempt and the fly landed at the base of the pool. Billy watched as a trout flashed in the sun and hit the fly.

"Keep the line tight and your rod tip up, but don't horse him in," Billy coached.

In spite of Ralph's frantic yelling and waving about, letting the line go slack and then falling down in the river, they managed to land the fish. Ralph whooped and hollered as he knelt in the water to hold his fish. "I can't wait to catch another one!"

They strung the fish with the others and put them in a shallow pool alongside the river. "I hope that bear isn't watching," said Billy. "No sharing with bears today. We need to catch two more so everybody will have a fish to eat."

Ralph grabbed the pole and waded up stream to the next pool. Billy watched his student proudly and remembered the patience his Dad had shown when he was learning. Of course, it helps if you catch fish. Ralph managed to catch another small one.

"Cast behind that big rock," Billy yelled. Ralph managed to

drape the line and fly over the rock where it caught momentarily on a clump of moss. The fly fell free and dropped into the water. There was a huge splash as a monster gobbled the fly and then disappeared under the rock. Ralph strained to pull the big fish out.

"Don't pull so hard," yelled Billy, "you'll break the leader. Give him some slack and maybe he'll swim out."

"Maybe I can scare him out with this stick," ventured Ralph. He picked up a stick and poked under the rock. The fish darted out and downstream. He leaped out of the water and then hit the end of the slack line. The leader snapped and the line went limp.

"We lost him. That fish must have been 25 inches and five pounds. I've never caught a fish that big," Billy said wistfully.

"What do we do now?" asked Ralph. "We've only caught six fish."

"Let's tie on our last royal coachman and catch number seven. We'll have to start up the trail soon, too," said Billy as he looked at his pocket watch.

Ralph took the rod and built a loop. He took one long back cast and brought the rod forward. The line accelerated toward the river and abruptly stopped.

"Ouch, Ralph, you hooked me!" screamed Billy. Ralph came quickly and saw the fly buried deeply in the back of Billy's neck.

"I guess I caught the seventh fish," laughed Ralph.

"It's not funny and besides it's our last royal coachman," Billy blurted out on the verge of tears.

They picked up the fish and their gear and mounted up. Billy still had the fly in his neck. The two horses were anxious to catch up to their friends so the pace was brisk. They would make camp by three.

After mucking through the bog and then a rest, the pack train started the ascent to Boulder cirque. The switchbacks were steep, but this time they were in looser dirt without the sharp rocks. There were clumps of aspen and willow clinging to the cliff side. Thistles grew at the trail edge and the horses strained to nip off the sticky blooms, sometimes leaning way over the steep edge.

Burt chided her horse Judy, "Is it worth our lives for that sticky, ant covered morsel?"

"You think she hears you or gives a damn?," Dougan called ahead.

They reached the top of the slope and, through a slot in the rock formation; Boulder Creek tumbled over the rocks in a delicate waterfall all the way down to the bog below. They were in the cirque. It was a wide hanging valley with a semicircle of mountain cliffs forming a backdrop. Clumps of alpine fir studded the meadow. Every wild flower in the mountains was in bloom. Clubs of bear grass lily remained in the meadow. Paintbrush in all shades of pink and red flamed in the grass. Spikes of lupine in shades of blue paired with yellow asters. Delicate lady slipper orchids stood in clumps along the creek. Gayfeather plumes protruded from rock crevices.

"What a beautiful garden!" exclaimed Burt? "Why can't we have something like this out on the prairie?"

"Then this wouldn't be so special," answered Sandy. "This is my favorite place in the mountain I'm glad I get to share it with you."

"The horses are anxious to get to the grass. Let's get to the campsite and unpack," urged W.D. "We will have to make a gate across the trail at the rock slot; then, we can turn them out."

They set up camp in a grove of alpine fir. Dougan climbed a tree and tied a long rope about 20 feet up. Sandy climbed another tree and tied the other end of the rope and pulled it tight. They draped a tarp over the line and tethered the corners to the other trees. "This will be our cooking and eating place. We could all get under if there's a storm," said Sandy.

W.D. and Kyle finished unpacking and unsaddling the horses. They turned them loose and the horses raced for the meadow. They kicked up their heels and bucked for joy. Several lay down to roll in the grass. The horse bells were ringing a symphony.

"This place is like a huge cathedral, only more beautiful," said Dougan with a reverent tone.

"What cathedrals have you seen?" asked Burt.

"Every city in Europe has a cathedral and I saw a lot of them. I saw Notre Dame, Westminster, St. Peters, St. Marks to name the famous ones," replied Dougan.

"Why didn't you stay over there if it was so great?," said Sandy sarcastically.

"Like I said, this is the most spectacular and I've got my reasons," retorted Dougan.

Sandy pulled out his watch. "Those boys should be getting to camp soon; it's after 3:00 o'clock."

No sooner had Sandy spoke, they saw two riders coming up the trail. "We're over here," Burt called. "Did you see Grandpa and Uncle Kyle back at the slot building a gate?"

The boys rode up and unloaded. "We caught breakfast!" exclaimed Ralph, "and I caught Billy."

They took the catch to the spring and packed the trout in cold water under a bundle of grass. They then recounted their fishing adventure.

"It's always the big one that gets away," Sandy said with false sympathy. "Let's take a look at the wounded Isaac Walton."

They all examined the fly deeply embedded in Billy's

neck. "I'll go get the pliers from the pack. We can push the fly through the other side, cut off the barbed point and take it out. It might hurt a bit," said Sandy.

"But Dad, that will ruin the fly and that is my last royal coachman," lamented Billy.

Dougan came over and examined the wound. "I think I can get it out without destroying the fly. It's still going to hurt. Do you have a tool with a long, sharp point or maybe a big fish hook?"

They scrambled through the tools and tackle. Sandy found a #2 hook. "I was saving that one for a big Dolly Varden trout when we get to Big River."

"I don't think I'll damage the big hook," speculated Dougan. "Now, let's get Billy's neck cleaned up. I'll need a piece of string or leader."

Dougan washed the blood and dirt from Billy's neck. He then tied a loop through the curve of the hook. "Put some gentle pull on the leader," he told Sandy. He then slid the point of the big hook alongside the fly hook.

"If I can get the point of the bigger hook into the recess behind the fly's barb, we might be able to back the fly out," said Dougan hopefully.

Billy yelped as the point went in and was wiggled around in the tissue. "You better save that fly is all I can say. This hurts a bit."

The probing point finally seated in the fly's barb. "Now let's back them out together, very slowly," cautioned Dougan.

Gently, the leader was pulled. There was a momentary hesitation and then the fly popped free. Everybody cheered.

"We better clean out that hole. Don't want you getting lockjaw," said Burt.

Billy was more interested in cleaning up the fly, but he let his mother clean out the wound.

"Better put some horse liniment on it," said Sandy.

"Ouch; Sun River Bridge!" said Billy as the stinging liniment touched the wound.

"What did you say, son?" said Sandy. "Saying that euphemism is not much better than the original. I don't want to hear it again."

"Sorry, Dad. I'll be good."

Dougan announced, "Dinner will be in two hours — time for a nap, gathering wood or making up your beds."

Billy and Ralph went off to gather wood, Sandy stretched out on his bedroll and went to sleep and W.D. and Kyle were off building a gate and checking the perimeter of the cirque. Burt went to her saddle bags and got out a book. It was Longfellow's poems — the book that had appeared on the kitchen counter. She sat down on the ground and leaned against a tree. She watched Dougan getting ready for the evening meal. She felt guilty for not getting up to help, yet she cherished this moment of respite. She was still saddle sore and more than a little sleep deprived. She tried to read a few verses of "Evangeline," but returned her gaze to Dougan. He was busy getting the kitchen organized. He built a fire pit and put the steel grate and tripod over the pit. He got out the pans, Dutch oven and eating dishes. He next laid the fire and started it, waiting for more wood. He glanced around and saw Burt staring at him. She quickly returned to her book.

She saw a new side of Dougan today, worldly, skilled, yet secretive. She also noticed that he was the only man in camp to shave and wash his hands. What was behind those steel blue eyes? He had always brushed her off when she quizzed him about his past. Maybe up here in the mountains he would feel safe enough to reveal his secrets.

She heard the boys coming in with wood and had to move when the smoke drifted her way. She walked into the cooking area and watched Dougan measuring out rice for the pot. "What's for dinner?" she said, trying to start a conversation.

"Just plain Spanish rice with sausage," returned Dougan. "If the hunters in the crowd would bring home some meat, we could have something heartier," he said in the direction of Billy and Ralph. "Maybe we could have a salad too; I saw some likely looking greens near the creek. Come with me and help."

Burt got up and glanced around. Sandy was snoring and Billy and Ralph were off gathering more wood. They walked to the creek and found some young dandelion, lamb's quarters, wild chives and miner's lettuce.

"These should make a wonderful salad," pronounced Dougan. "I'll dress them with some bacon fryings, vinegar and sugar."

Burt was amazed. "I didn't know you were a gourmet chef. You ate my plain fare all summer and never complained. You even complimented occasionally."

"A good meal is mostly the company, and I sure enjoy your company," returned Dougan.

"And likewise, Mr. Dougan."

When they got back to camp, everybody was there.

Burt, slightly embarrassed, took charge. "Look at these great greens! We're going to have a fine salad to go with the great Spanish rice. I hope you're all hungry. Billy could you and Ralph fill those pans with water and put them on to boil?"

She glanced at Dougan while he prepared the rice, canned tomatoes, chili powder and sausage chunks. He dug out the can of bacon grease from breakfast and re-melted it on the fire. He seemed to float about the campsite getting everything to come together at once.

Everyone grabbed a plate and tin cup and stood in line waiting for the feast. Dougan quickly mixed the hot bacon grease, vinegar and salt and drenched the greens.

"Do you want to say a blessing, Billy?" said Dad.

They all took off their hats as Billy prayed, "Dear God,

thank you for the mountains, for my friends, for Mom, Dad and sisters and for this food. Amen."

"Dig in," said Dougan.

"That was the best Spanish rice I've ever eaten," raved Ralph. "I even liked the salad."

"Everything tastes better in the mountains, but thank you," replied Dougan. "And now, you can help with the dishes."

The late twilight seemed to make the high walls around the cirque glow. Grandpa pointed to a small herd of mountain goats traversing a high ledge above them. "We're here in crazy Jacques La Fleur's country. Be on the lookout tonight."

"Tell us about it, Grandpa," begged Billy.

"That's a tale for the campfire," teased W.D.

The fire blazed up and sparks streaked toward the emerging stars. The alpine sky was purple black; the planets were brilliant lights on the horizon. W.D. lit his pipe and drew out the suspense. A wolf howled in the distance.

"Hear that wolf. That's probably old Jacques La Fleur. When I came out here in '78, crazy Jacques was a legend. He was a French Indian trapper who roamed the front lands and this area of the mountains. He was a loner, but seemed to have a special communication with the wildlife. He could call a wolf right up to his camp before he killed it for the bounty and the hide. The Indians said he took on the spirit of his kills. Whenever there was a wolf kill of an animal, the spirit of Jacques was blamed. He was even blamed for disappearances of humans. They once found a dead man just over that ridge that had his liver torn out and eaten. There were man tracks all around. The legend goes on that he lived in a cave just over that ridge and that an old she-bear lived there too. They shared their kills."

"What happened to him, Grandpa?" asked Billy.

"No one knows for sure. There's a grave at the top of Crazy Creek Pass some say belongs to Jacques, but others say he's still alive in the form of a bear or wolf. The Indians believe he haunts this area and they avoid coming here."

Just then, the wolf howled again. "That is Jacques now," whispered Grandpa. "He's hungry for liver tonight — especially, a 12-year-old liver."

They all got up to go to bed. "Let's sleep close to the fire," whispered Ralph to Billy.

The ground shook with stomping. Snorts and grunts came from the bushes and the noises of crashing of brush filled the night. Billy sat up and yelled, "there's a bear in camp!" It was incredibly noisy for the usually quiet night. No one wanted to get up and confront a bear. Finally, Sandy got up and went to the still glowing fire and threw on some kindling. In the dim light, eyes lit in the distance. Then, more crashing and stomping. "Relax everybody, it's a couple of deer fighting through camp," said Sandy.

"What time is it, Dad?" asked Billy.

"It's 3 o'clock. It will be light in an hour." They all looked at the incredible night sky. In the high altitude, it looked like a zillion stars filled the sky. As they watched, a large meteor streaked from mountain rim to rim.

"I guess we should thank those deer for waking us to see this magnificent display," said Burt.

"Go back to sleep, Burt, or get up and make some coffee," said Sandy.

Dawn streaked across the eastern sky. It was 4 A.M. The campers could see their breath in the pale light and were reluctant to leave their warm bed rolls, but no one could get back to sleep. Dougan finally got up and stoked the fire to life. He put on water to boil and made coffee. Soon, others came to the fire.

"Did it freeze? It sure feels like it," commented Sandy.

"There was a skin of ice on the water in the wash basin," said Dougan.

Soon everyone was cradling a tin cup of hot coffee and hunching over the fire. Dawn comes early, but the sun doesn't break into the cirque for a few hours. They could see the sunlight reflecting off the tip of the surrounding peaks.

"Hey you, fisherman. Let's have trout for breakfast. I'll make biscuits and you cook the fish, okay?" said Dougan.

Billy and Ralph retrieved the fish from the spring and re-washed them. They were stiff and cold, but still beautiful. "We only have six, so two can share the biggest one," Billy said proudly.

Dougan had the big cast iron skillet on the fire and the lard was crackling. The biscuits were in the Dutch oven. "Time to flour the fish and fry them," instructed Dougan. "Just dredge the whole fish in this seasoned flour and drop him in the pan. Don't splash the grease."

Billy and Ralph hovered over the frying fish, squinting their eyes when the smoke drifted in their faces. "It is time to turn them?" said Ralph.

Dougan lifted the fish and saw the golden brown crust. "Yes, turn them. Be gentle; we don't have scrambled fish on the menu today."

Billy lifted the trout out of the pan and on to a tin plate. "Come and get it!" he called, even though the whole group was already standing around in anticipation.

Sandy gave a demonstration on de-boning a cooked trout. He held the tail with his left hand and gently broke the crust of the skin at the tail. Then, he lifted with the tail and pushed the flesh off half the fish and stripped off the other half. He then held up the skeleton, free of flesh and tossed it into the fire. Two perfect fillets lay on his plate. Dougan plopped a biscuit beside and Sandy took a bite. "Eat'em while they're hot.

They cool off fast on these tin plates."

They all tried de-boning with varying success.

"Good job on the fish, boys," praised W.D., "but we'll expect two apiece next time."

After breakfast, they planned out the day. "We'll stay here one more night. Today is a free day; explore the area, take a nap, catch a horse and go for a ride, do some target practice with the rifles or climb the ridge and look over the continental divide" announced Sandy.

Billy and Ralph decided they would go hunting and exploring, Sandy and Kyle would climb to the top of Corrugated Ridge. Dougan wanted to explore the forest. Burt and Grandpa said they would stay in camp and make lunch or take a nap. "We'll all meet here by 1:00 o'clock," said Sandy.

Billy and Ralph took the .22 and walked up the trail that eventually climbed out of the cirque to Crazy Creek Pass. They climbed through some stunted firs and then emerged above the timberline on a rock strewn plateau that had been planed off by the glacier. They saw a few ground squirrels standing erect and chirping their warning. Billy loaded the .22 and squeezed off a shot. The bullet ricocheted off a rock and whined off into the ravine below. The squirrel disappeared. "My turn next," begged Ralph.

"If you kill it, you have to eat it," said Billy.

"If you had killed that squirrel, would you have eaten it?" asked Ralph.

"Maybe so," said Billy. "It's okay if you're shooting a varmint that does damage like a chicken killing weasel or skunk — you don't have to eat those."

"Then let's shoot something we can eat," said Ralph. They walked along the ridge and came upon a pile of rocks with a cross stuck in it.

"This must be crazy Jacques' grave!" said Ralph as he hesitantly approached.

"Be careful, we don't want to stir him up. We're trespassing on his territory now," cautioned Billy. They backed up and then turned and ran back down the trail.

"Let's go back to that brush and scrub. Maybe our dinner is in there!" said Billy. As they neared the brush, they heard a drumming sound. "I think that's a grouse." Carefully, they crept to the edge of the thicket and then peered in. They saw the grouse sitting on a downed log getting ready to drum again. Without saying a word, Billy took off the safety and leveled the gun at the bird. He wanted a head shot so as not to ruin any meat. He would either kill the bird or miss entirely. He let out his breath and squeezed the trigger. The grouse toppled off the log.

"You hit it!" exclaimed Ralph. "My turn next." They walked to the dead bird and Billy put it in a sock tied it to his belt.

"It seems kind of small, not enough for seven," said Ralph as he examined the bird.

"We'll just have to get some more," returned Billy.

They heard another grouse drumming in the distance as they cautiously picked their way through the scrub. Then, they saw a grouse walking down the trail in front of them only a few feet away.

"That's a fool hen," said Billy. "It thinks it's invisible to us."

Ralph shouldered the rifle and squeezed off a shot. The bird dropped in its tracks. "That was too easy. I see why they call them fool hens. What's their real name?"

"Dad calls them Franklin's grouse, whoever Franklin is," said Billy "Now everybody can have a taste, but one more bird would be nice."

They walked into another thicket but jumped back as a big bull elk crashed out of his day bed and charged across the meadow toward camp. He was shedding the last of his velvet. "That's what Dad calls a rag horn," Billy explained. "That bull would make a handsome trophy. Dad has hunted back here for many years and has never shot one that big."

No sooner had the big bull left, they saw another grouse. Ralph had the rifle, so he drew a bead and then they had three. They walked back into camp with their trophies.

Dougan had been out exploring the meadow. He found some clumps of wild onion and dug them up with his sheath knife. At the edge of the forest, he found some fresh mushrooms. He carefully inspected them; no shroud, pink gills, smooth top, no worms. I think these are edible, he said to himself. He chewed a small piece and it tasted delicious. These look like the mushrooms we ate back in France. He gathered his shirt tail full of onions and mushrooms and started back for camp. As he stepped around a large downed log, he found Burt reclining, reading a book. He cleared his throat, but still startled her.

She gasped and choked out, "I thought you were a bear!."

"Sorry, Burt. What are you reading?"

"Just a book of Longfellow's poems that mysteriously appeared in my kitchen a few months ago. It really brings back the memories of my early teaching years," said Burt wistfully.

"What is your favorite Longfellow poem?" asked Dougan.

"That's a hard decision, but I'd have to choose *Evangeline*. It has drama, intrigue, unrequited love and beautiful passages. I cry every time I read it. I used to have my students memorize portions and sometimes reenact the scenes," she related.

"Do you ever feel like Evangeline?" he asked.

"I suppose every woman feels like Evangeline on occasion; disrupted from her comfort zone, dreaming of what might have been," she confessed, "and what of you, Mr. Dougan, do you feel like Gabriel?."

"I could be Gabriel; wandering, just missing the prize."

"Is there an Evangeline waiting somewhere?"

"There was one a long time ago, but she's gone. I'm still looking for Evangeline."

"Well, Mr. Jack Dougan, you're not going to find her out here in the wilds of Montana. That's not why you're here. Just why are you here?" quizzed Burt.

"To keep you guessing and to be around you. I know we've got a connection," he said with exaggerated emphasis.

"Teasing will get you nowhere, Jack. I'm serious, why are you running?" she pleaded.

"I'm sorry, Burt. I didn't mean to belittle your question, but I'm not ready to open up to anyone. Why can't we just have a pleasant moment together?"

"You better be getting back to camp. The boys will be looking for you," Burt ordered. Dougan gathered his mushrooms and onions and walked into camp just as the rest of the party was straggling in. Sandy and Kyle had made it all the way to the top of Corrugated Ridge. W.D. had checked out the horses and the barricade on the trail and the boys were walking in carrying some kind of trophy.

Billy and Ralph walked up to the camp table and tossed the dead grouse on top. "We killed dinner," bragged the boys.

"Great!" responded Dougan, "but you boys expect us to eat feathers and all? A good hunter dresses his game and cleans his fish. You've had your fun; now the hard work," said Dougan sternly.

They were somewhat surprised when the birds were handed back to them. "Bring them back ready for the pot while I get the rest of the ingredients together," Dougan said cheerfully.

The boys set out to pluck and draw the grouse. "This is way harder than it looks," said Ralph as he blew the feathers off his hand.

"Mom always scalded the chickens before plucking them," said Billy, "but I never had to help."

They finally finished plucking and then came the drawing.

"Just cut across the belly and pull out the guts," Billy ordered.

"You do it," said Ralph with a squeamish look on his face.

Billy took his sheath knife and made the cut. He cut too deep and spilled the gut contents. The birds were still warm and the smell got to Ralph who had to go behind a tree and retch. Billy managed to eviscerate the bird and then reached inside to extract the heart and lungs. "One done, two to go," he panted. "Your turn, Chief Weak Stomach."

Ralph shakily took the knife and gingerly cut through the belly skin. The entrails came out clean and easy. "That's how you do it," he bragged.

They finished the last bird and took them to the spring to rinse off the spillage and blood. In the meantime, Dougan had started the stew. He put in mushrooms, onions, carrots, salt and pepper. He rummaged through the pack and found his treasury of spices and herbs. He put in garlic and a bit of Tabasco. He was secretive about his cooking. He cut up the grouse into individual pieces and added them to the mix. Finally, he got out the cooking wine and poured half a bottle into the pot. "I've got to save some for a trout dish that's on my menu," he murmured. He covered the pot and moved it to a cooler part of the fire grate. "This needs to cook slowly for a couple of hours," he said to no one.

Burt came strolling into camp. "I smell something good. What's for dinner?" she sang.

"No looking in the pot," scolded Dougan. "It's a surprise."

Billy found his Dad, "Let's go target shooting before dinner."

"Let's all go," said Grandpa.

Sandy, Kyle, W.D. and the two boys grabbed their guns and walked over the ridge. Billy was hoping he would be allowed to shoot Grandpa's pistol or Dad's deer rifle. They found a nice level spot to shoot from and a nice bank to shoot into.

"Find us some targets," said the men.

Ralph went back to camp to gather any empty tin cans

while Billy scrounged the woods for small logs and big leaves. They set up the targets about 100 feet away. Billy lined up several small rocks on top of a fallen tree and set the tin cans in a row at the base of the log.

"You first, Billy," said Dad. "One shot standing, one kneeling and one prone, and here, use the .30-.30."

Billy carefully took the rifle. It was a lever action Winchester, saddle carbine model 1894 with open hammer. It had belonged to Grandpa before he gave it to Dad. Someday, it would be his. "How many deer has this rifle killed?" asked Billy.

"Quite a few," replied Grandpa, "plus coyotes, badgers and a couple of elk."

Billy ratcheted the lever and saw the shiny brass round entering the chamber. He carefully released the hammer and stood ready for his first shot. He tried to remember the whole sequence Dad had taught him, plus all the "never" and "always" warnings. He leveled the rifle, exhaled, cocked the hammer and squeezed the trigger. Crack went the gun and the echo bounced around the cirque for 10 seconds. He heard the whine of the ricochet and saw the target still standing.

"I guess I missed," said Billy. "That was quite a kick."

"Two more shots," said Dad.

Billy dropped to one knee. He braced his elbow on his knee and carefully took aim. Crack! The little rock on the log exploded and everybody cheered. Billy hit the next rock from the prone position.

"Look out deer and elk," said Grandpa, "we've got another sharpshooter in the family."

"Your turn, Dad," said Billy as he handed the rifle back to Sandy. There's an empty in the chamber, but we always assume the gun is loaded, right Dad?"

Sandy reloaded. A new trio of rocks rested on the log. He stood on the rise and brought the rifle to his shoulder. Bang!

Ratchet; bang! Ratchet; bang! Three shots in two seconds. All three rocks disappeared and the mountains were still reverberating.

"Mighty fancy shooting for a dirt farmer, brother," said Kyle. "You were always the best shot, even before you went off to military academy."

They all tried a few shots and then W.D. got out his pistol. "Move those cans closer, about 50 feet," he ordered.

Billy and Ralph scrambled to set up the targets. Both were hoping they would get to shoot the pistol. W.D. took the .45 in both hands and aimed the pistol. He shot three quick shots. Then, he tried from the hip. As he ejected the casings, he said, "I'm getting a little rusty; only five out of six."

"Can I try, Grandpa?" pleaded Billy.

W.D. started the instruction patiently explaining the revolver's mechanism, the hammer, trigger and ejector. They reloaded together.

"Hold the gun with both hands, lock your wrists, slowly bring the barrel down on your target and line up the sights. Exhale and steadily squeeze the trigger. Try not to pull to the side as you squeeze. Be prepared for the recoil which will lift the muzzle up and back," cautioned W.D.

Billy took the revolver as Grandpa had instructed. It was heavy. As he tried to come down on the target, the muzzle swayed all around. He repositioned and exhaled. The bang and recoil surprised him. He saw the dust kick up several feet from the can. "This is harder than it looks; can I try again?"

The next three shots were progressively closer and, finally, they heard the cling of the tin can.

"One out of six ain't bad, but you wouldn't have gotten that outlaw before he got you," teased W.D.

"How did you get so good?" asked Billy.

"Lot of practice," assured W.D.

Dougan walked up. "It sounded like a war going on. I

thought I might get in on the action." Dougan pulled a sling shot out of his back pocket. "I used to be pretty good with one of these. I managed to get some genuine latex rubber tubing that came all the way from India."

Everyone stood back as Dougan selected a few stones from the ground. He took aim and let it fly. Pling went the tin can as it bounced from the hit. Pling went the next can and then the third can before Dougan missed.

"Who needs a gun when you're as good a shot as you!" exclaimed Billy. "Where did you learn to do that?"

"Back when I was your age in Illinois. I even managed to take down a coon or two. By the way, you warriors, dinner is ready. Time to wash up and get ready."

They all headed back to camp. Billy dreamed of being as good as shot as his Dad and Grandpa — maybe having his own pistol some day to wear with his goat hair chaps and leather vest. He wondered if he could be as good at everything as Dad — how long it would take?

Billy filled the wash basins with hot water from the camp-fire and cold from the spring. Everybody washed up and then stood around the fire drinking coffee. Billy and Ralph put lots of canned milk in theirs. Dougan had made a makeshift table out of logs and the pack boxes and a tablecloth out of two pannier tarps. He set out the pan of fresh biscuits, a big bowl of mushroom rice and a bowl of greens. He then took the lid off the stew pot. Everybody drooled at the smell that wafted from the pot.

Sandy took off his hat and offered blessing. "Oh, Lord, thank you for this food and for our time together in Your wonderful creation. Amen." Hats went back on and everybody dished up.

"I must say, Mr. Dougan, this is the finest grouse stew that I have ever tasted, from Chicago to San Francisco," raved W.D.

"It's called *coq au vin*," replied Dougan, "something I picked up in my travels."

"Well, cock-a-doodle-doo to you too, but it's still chicken stew," cracked Sandy.

Burt chimed in, "I think that is chicken with wine in French, right Dougan?"

"*Oui, oui,* Madame," said Dougan with a bow.

"You got a fancy name for these biscuits, too?" piped Billy.

"It's just good grub," answered Ralph, "shut up and eat."

They cleaned their plates, the pot and all the biscuits. "That was good!" exclaimed Sandy. "Dougan, you'd make someone a good wife."

The sun dropped behind Corrugated Ridge, but all the mountain tops were still warmly lit. Huge towering pink and orange clouds loomed on the eastern horizon.

"We might get a thundershower tonight," commented Sandy. "Kyle and I saw thunderheads all across the prairie from the top of Corrugated Ridge today. Billy, you and Ralph go catch two horses so we can use them to round up the rest tomorrow morning. We'll be breaking camp and should be on the trail by 10 o'clock."

Billy saw the horses on the far side of the valley. He went to the pack boxes and grabbed a handful of oats and a carrot, then headed for the herd. He whistled for Pedro and yelled his name. They heard the horse bells tinkling and Pedro and Judy trotting towards them. Pedro muzzled Billy's pocket for the treats. Billy slipped the lead rope around Pedro's neck and then gave him the carrot. Ralph caught Judy and they led them to a stump so they could mount bareback. When they got to camp, the dishes were done and everybody was sitting around the fire telling stories.

They tied up the horses and joined the campfire group. "Tell us about the war, Dougan; did you kill any Germans?" asked Billy.

Everybody went silent waiting for Dougan's reply. Dougan poked a stick into the fire and pulled it out to light a cigarette. "That's a chapter in my life I'd like to forget," he said apologetically.

"And where did you learn to cook like that?" quizzed Kyle.

"What's this? Twenty questions for Dougan?" he said as he winked at Burt across the fire.

W.D. passed out cigars for the four men. He offered one to Burt. "Would that make me one of the boys?" she quipped.

"Isn't that what you want?" W.D. said sarcastically.

She stood up. "I'm going to bed so you can tell your stories and not have to tone them down because of me," she quipped.

It was nearly dark. The tall thunderclouds on the horizon would occasionally glow from internal lightning. They heard a wolf howl in the distance, but all else was quiet.

* * *

They were awakened by brilliant flashes of lightning that illuminated the entire cirque. Booms of thunder bounced off the reef and down the canyons. Billy and Ralph pulled the tarps over their sleeping bags. They watched a lightning strike on the ridge and, after the ear splitting crack of thunder, heard the rock fall as a slide cascaded down the cliff face.

"This is the wildest lightning show I've ever seen!" exclaimed Ralph.

Then, a few big drops of rain rattled the trees and tarps. Billy pulled the tarp over his head. More drops, and then a deluge. Water was rushing down the gullies and filled the low spot where they were sleeping.

"I'm soaked," said Billy, "we've got to move to higher ground."

"We can't get any wetter; we could just stay here," added Ralph.

"Let's go up under the cooking shelter when the rain lets up," said Billy.

When they dragged their wet bedrolls and tarps to the shelter, they found the rest of the party already there. They crowded in beside Mom and Dad.

"We'll get early start come daylight," called Dougan. "Anybody want to start the fire now and drink coffee until dawn?"

"That's fine with me," said Burt. "I can't stand another minute in this wet sack."

Dougan got up and stirred the ash pile. A few live embers glowed in the dark. He had some drier kindling stacked at the base of a nearby tree. Soon, the fire was blazing and the soggy campers huddled around.

"I'm glad it rained so hard," said Sandy. "There's less chance of a lightning strike fire now. These woods are mighty dry."

After a couple cups of coffee, the eastern sky started to lighten. A coyote yelped at the dawn and the ravens replied with a rattly caw.

A new day had arrived.

Chapter XIII

By the time the sun broke into the high hanging valley, the early risers had finished breakfast and were packing up. Billy and Sandy took Pedro and Judy and rode off to find the horses. They finally heard the tinkling bells in a stand of timber.

"They probably took shelter during the storm," Sandy said. "It looks like they're all here."

Sandy rode up beside Wolf and grabbed his halter. Billy caught Punch. "We've got the leaders; let's head for camp via the slot so we can take the fence down," said Sandy.

"Dad, were you scared last night during the storm?" Billy asked.

"A little," replied Sandy. "Lightning is a powerful and fickle phenomenon. Remember the cow and two calves that were killed over at the south pasture last year? Or the fires that were started by lightning? I hope last night's storm didn't start any fires up here."

"There was too much rain for a fire to start," said Billy.

"I hope you're right. Sometimes, lightning will strike an old stump and it will smolder for days. Then, a wind will fan it alive and a forest fire starts. There's a fire lookout atop Mount Wright that can see the whole area and send a crew to put out a little fire before it becomes a big one," Sandy explained.

When they got back to camp with the horses, most of the pack boxes were filled and the wet bed rolls stacked and ready for loading. The horses were saddled and the pack horses loaded. Billy watched carefully as Dad threw the diamond hitches and cinched them down. "Next time, let me do it," begged Billy.

"Okay, son. Soon you will be leading the mountain pack trips at the rate you're going," assured Sandy.

Sandy mounted and took the tow line for four pack horses. Kyle took the other string. Sandy shouted back, "Give us ten 10 minutes lead and we will meet at the pass."

The other riders filled their saddle bags and tied on their wet slickers. Billy and Ralph had kept their fishing gear out of the packs and they tied the poles along the front skirt and fenders of the saddles where a rifle scabbard would go.

"Time to go," yelled W.D.

"Can I give you a leg up?" Dougan said to Burt as he locked his hands to form a stirrup.

Burt stepped up, but hesitated before swinging up. She rested her hand on Dougan's shoulder and brushed his cheek as she swung up. She felt his hand on her thigh as he stood up and held the stirrup. Her heart was racing and she felt a flush. "Thank you, Mr. Dougan," she said as she relaxed in the saddle. She began rehearsing the scenarios before her.

Billy watched the exchange and felt embarrassed that he hadn't offered to help his mother. She was doing quite well on the trip and was becoming a better horse rider. Maybe she would take it up after they got back; maybe get her own horse.

Grandpa led the group up the switchbacks climbing out of the cirque. They could see Crazy Horse Pass above them. The pack horse strings were just tiny figures near the summit. Billy and Ralph rode in the middle while Burt and Dougan followed. As they passed each other on each switchback, Billy could hear the bantering small talk between Mother and Dougan. Mom seemed more talkative and chipper today.

Near the summit, they passed by the pile of rocks that marked Jacques La Fleur's grave. Grandpa stopped, dismounted and walked to the grave. The winter storms had knocked over the cross. Grandpa stood it up and piled more rocks around the base of the cross. "We don't need the ghost of crazy Jacques to be haunting us," he joked. From there, they could see the summit and the snow bank that had formed in the lee of the pass. The advanced group was at the edge of the bank letting their horses drink the snow melt. When they got to the pass, they were nearly knocked off their horses by the wind that funneled through the notch. They scrambled down to the snow bank and watered their horses.

"Let's have a snow ball fight!" yelled Billy as he walked onto the snow. The icy mass would only yield big crystals he scraped up, but he still managed to shower everybody with snow.

"I could have used some cooling off yesterday, but its cold up here this morning and I've still got damp clothes on," complained Ralph.

"Throw me some snow; I could use some cooling off," Burt said as she glanced at Dougan.

"Hang onto your hats; we're going through the pass," yelled Sandy as the pack trains went on ahead. Below them was a wide "U" shaped valley with bare rock sides. To the north, they could see continuing ranges of snow capped peaks and to the east they could see out onto the plains. Crazy Creek was a silver thread way below. The trail started the traverse over the steep rockslide on the flank of Mount Patrick Gass. W.D. explained to them the mountain had been renamed, just recently, after Sergeant Patrick Gass, one of the Lewis and Clark expedition men.

The trail was steep and rocky. The horses skidded and jerked as they descended. At several points, the three groups were almost stacked on each other as they zigzagged down the steep slope. Burt again felt the pressure of the saddle tree and wondered if this was a test of the devil. She hadn't been this excited since her wedding night and that was mostly anticipation. Should she let herself go and risk falling off the horse or making a sound? Was Dougan to blame? He obviously was infatuated too.

"Why so silent, Burt? Are you afraid of tumbling down the rockslide?" yelled Dougan.

"No, I'm just daydreaming," she replied.

"About what if I might ask?"

"About things; the future, the ranch, tonight, my wet gear, and my men," she sighed.

"Pretty big stuff. You must feel like the queen bee with six men around you," he returned.

"Maybe six good for nothing drones," she teased.

They reached the valley floor and entered a wide stand of fuchsia colored fireweed. It was almost too colorful to absorb. Hundreds of bees were busy gathering nectar. The flowers were up to their stirrups or higher.

"Have you ever seen anything this spectacular?" commented Dougan. "I'd like to roll in the flowers."

"The bees may give you some points to remember," laughed Burt.

"I was thinking of the two of us rolling in the flowers," Dougan said with a big grin.

"Now that wouldn't be romantic at all," quipped Burt. "Bees and rocks and sticker bushes. You'd have to be mighty desperate."

"Maybe I am," returned Dougan.

They continued down the trail and entered a grove of trees. The shade felt good. They could hear the roar of Crazy Creek down below them, but couldn't see the stream. Then, they broke into the open and looked down a 50-foot-deep chasm to the rushing creek below. About a mile further down the trail, they came to the South Fork of Birch Creek. Crazy Creek joined Birch Creek at a nice wide gravel bar.

"This is good place for lunch," said Sandy as he dismounted. The horses drank deeply as did the riders. Everybody sprawled on the gravel bar as Dougan unpacked lunch. He opened a can of Vienna sausages and opened the large stack of leftover pancakes from breakfast.

"Lunch is served," said Dougan with a slight bow. Even the dry pancake with the sausage tasted good in the mountain air. "What's for dessert?" said Billy.

Dougan got off his haunches and opened the pack. He rummaged around and came up with seven Hershey bars. "Now this is gourmet," he commented. "I stayed up all night to make these."

Sandy commented, "It's about two hours to camp on Big River Meadows. Dougan, Kyle and I will go now and we can set up camp. Grandpa can bring the rest of you later if you would like to stay here for a nap or fishing or exploring."

"Fishing!" yelled Billy. "I saw a trout back at the ford with my name on him."

"I'll stay here and take a nap. Nobody got much sleep last night," said W.D.

"Me, too," echoed Burt.

Billy and Ralph rigged up their fishing equipment while W.D. and Burt rolled out their damp bed rolls to dry out in the sun. When the boys were out of earshot, W.D. addressed Burt, "Well, what do you think of a mountain pack trip with the men?"

Burt studied W.D. and replied, "The scenery is fantastic, but the accommodations are a little rustic. Why do you ask?"

"I was thinking there must be another reason you would want to rough it up here."

"You mean so I wouldn't have to take a bath, cook for the haying crew, or be left behind to do the chores?" she snapped.

"Now don't be sarcastic," said W.D. "I was just making polite conversation."

"You don't like me up here butting in on the stag party, do you?" she challenged.

"I didn't say that," he replied.

She interrupted, "In fact, you don't like me much anyway."

"You're my son's wife and my grandchildren's mother, so I have no choice but to like you," he smiled.

"You think I married Sandy for his money and the ranch; you thought I was a desperate old maid," she blurted with vehemence.

"You must be feeling guilty or sorry for yourself," replied W.D. "You signed up to be a rancher's wife. This is part of the deal."

Burt picked up her things and walked away before she said something that would really start a war.

She found a secluded spot in view of the creek. She lay there gathering her thoughts. Did the old man sense her feelings for Dougan? Did she really marry Sandy for his money? Would she have been an old maid school teacher? No, she was the heroine of the story. She had spurned lovers, had a great adventure, married a young rancher, had three beautiful children and was now on another great adventure. She had practically raised Sandy and had guided him in his ranching success. She felt she could run it all if need be. "I can do anything," she mused.

She heard Billy calling, "Mom, it's time to head out."

She gathered her still damp bedroll and walked to the horses. W.D. and the boys were untying the horses and tightening the cinches. She lashed on her bedroll and Billy gave her a leg up.

"We caught more fish for dinner," beamed Billy. "Ralph caught the biggest one."

Birch Creek Canyon wound up toward the Continental Divide on an easy incline as opposed to the switchbacks of Blackleaf and Crazy Creek passes. There were two noisy waterfalls they skirted and some stands of dense regrowth lodgepole pines they nearly had to bushwhack through.

They crested a small rim and Grandpa announced, "This is Gateway Pass. The Continental Divide. Spit on the ground here and half will run down the Missouri and Mississippi to the Gulf of Mexico and the other half will run into the Columbia and the Pacific Ocean."

"Have you been to those places?" Billy asked as he spit on the ground.

"To the Atlantic and Pacific, but not to the Gulf" responded W.D.

Burt chimed in, "Remember about Louisiana when we read *It's on the Gulf*?"

"I don't need to go there, but I would like to see the ocean sometime," said Billy with a smile.

They came to a fence line with a closed gate across the trail. "This fence separates the livestock up here on forest service grazing permits. When we get through the gate, we'll be on Johnny Sabado's range. The fence will also keep our horses from escaping back the way we've come."

"How much further to camp?," asked Burt. "I'm ready for a break."

"Only about 30 minutes; can you make it that long?" needled W.D.

Billy got off and opened the gate and closed it behind the party. They were down the trail only a few minutes when they heard the horses calling each other. Then, they saw the smoke plume from the campfire and soon they entered Big River Meadows. The open grassy meadow spread across the valley. It was about two miles long and one mile wide. It was an old lake bed, drained when Gateway Creek cut through the moraine at Gateway Gorge. It was a perfect grazing area for all kinds of critters. A brush lined creek meandered down the center. As they approached the camp, they smelled a sweet, fruity fragrance. "Its huckleberry!" yelled Billy. "We can have huckleberry pancakes!"

"You boys can come back for the berries. I'm ready for camp," said Burt.

Camp was already set up at the edge of the forest. The cooking shelter was strung out. Bedrolls were hung on the lines to dry. The horses were grazing in the meadow and the forward party was stretched out under the trees.

"About time you got here. I'm sorry you missed dinner. You'll have to fend for yourself," said Dougan solemnly.

"We've got a few fish; too bad you've already eaten the beans. You could have had fish," joked Billy.

"Put up your horses and I'll see what we can round up for dinner," said Dougan.

The horses raced for the tall grass. Some rolled in the meadow. The horse bells rang a syncopated cacophony.

Billy and Ralph could smell dinner cooking all the way from the horse compound. They hurriedly tied up the saddles in trees so the salt craving creatures wouldn't get to the saddles, cinches or horse blankets.

"That smells so good it'll attract all the bears in the wilderness!" exclaimed Ralph.

They got to camp in time to see the biscuits coming out of the Dutch oven. Dougan was slicing up a big country ham and Kyle was stirring a pot of red eye gravy. Three cans of beans were side boiling in the coals.

"Don't kick ashes into the beans," warned Dougan, "and be sure you wash up — here's some soap." The boys went to the nearby stream to wash and to put their trout into the cool water. They could see small trout racing up and down the stream in alarm. "We should get up early and catch enough for breakfast," said Ralph.

"Let's go after supper," said Billy. "We'll have a couple of hours until dark."

Sandy said the blessing and everybody dished up their plates with ham slices, biscuits and gravy plus beans.

"Are baked beans a vegetable?" asked Billy.

"Up here in camp they are," said Burt. "Maybe you guys could find some more edible greens after dinner."

"We're going fishing," they said in unison. "Do you want to come along?"

"Not tonight. I'm going to stay near the fire and not get eaten up by the mosquitoes."

"I'll go with you," said Sandy. "I haven't caught a trout on this trip yet."

Kyle and W.D. decided they would go back up the trail and find the huckleberries. That left Dougan and Burt at camp to do the dishes and secure the grub.

Dougan washed the plates and cups in the Dutch oven full of hot soapy water. Burt rinsed them in the wash bucket full of boiling hot water and stacked them on an empty pack box to dry. The tin plates and cups were hot potatoes as she juggled them onto the drying rack.

"All the men should do dishes. That way, they'd get their hands clean," Burt said with an exasperated sigh. "Your hands are always clean and not so calloused and beat up as Sandy's."

"My hands are my living," replied Dougan. "Whether it's dealing cards, cooking or patching up wounds, I need my hands to be quick and nimble."

"That's the first you've mentioned about your past. Tell me more," she said with a flirting glance.

"I've been considering that. I probably do owe you an explanation. I haven't told anybody these things and it could be dangerous for me if the wrong people got wind of me or where I'm at," he replied.

"Don't put yourself at risk for my sake," she said, "but I am good at keeping confidences."

"I want to tell you. You mean a lot to me and we share a lot of the same dreams and fantasies," he sighed.

"Okay, I'm listening."

"I was born in Ohio. My father was an officer in the Army, so we traveled a lot. I was eight years old when he went off with Teddy Roosevelt to fight the Spanish-American War. He came back crippled, so we settled on a little farm in Ohio. I dreamed about being a doctor or lawyer or a politician. I didn't want to be a soldier or a farmer."

"It was my job to take care of the animals on the farm, so I milked the cow, fed the pigs and tended our two horses. We just got by on father's little pension and the farm's output. I wanted to go to college, but we were poor and I had to take care of mother and father. A local schoolteacher, just like you, introduced me to the classics and would read to me and loan me books from her library. She was my inspiration, just like you."

"I became friends with the local country doctor who came to the house frequently to take care of Father. He encouraged me to study with him. Back then, you could become a doctor through apprenticeship and taking the state examination. I studied with Doctor Brown for five years. We would make house calls together. He taught me to sew up wounds, deliver babies and splint broken bones."

"What happened then, why didn't you become a doctor?" Burt asked, still not fully believing the story.

"Father got sicker and I had to stay home more, so the apprenticeship slowed. I still studied whenever I could."

"How about your mother, couldn't she help?"

"Mother was an emotional wreck. She couldn't do anything but fret. I had to do most of the housework and the farm work, plus take care of Father."

"You must have been frustrated," Burt sympathized.

"To put it mildly! It was a relief when Father died, although we had to sell the farm to take care of the expenses."

"What happened to your mother?"

"She went to live with her sister in the Chicago area, and

the last I heard she was in a mental hospital. I haven't seen her in years."

"So you're an orphan?"

"Pretty much. This is the closest thing to family I've experienced. I didn't realize how much I missed family."

"Was there a woman in your life?" asked Burt.

"Yes. There was Molly Brown, the doctor's daughter. She was 17 and I was 25. Doc Brown thought we were too far apart or she was too young, so discouraged our romance. In fact, it almost halted my apprenticeship. Doc said if we still felt the same way when she was 20, then he might consider letting our relationship advance. I respected him so much that I sacrificed our love," he choked.

"What happened to Molly Brown?" ventured Burt.

"That's another chapter in a long, sad story," he said as he stirred the fire and threw on another log.

"Everybody is out fishing or gathering, you can talk," urged Burt.

"After Mom went off and the farm sold, I was free. The war had broken out in Europe and I thought I could use my doctoring skills or improve them in the Army, so I enlisted. They put me in the infantry and shipped me off to France."

"Out there, it was kill or be killed. I still have nightmares of the trenches, the constant artillery, the charges, the cold, wet, the lice, the stench, and the dead. I did get to practice my doctoring aplenty. They started calling me Doc as I performed battlefield first aid. I even did a couple of amputations. Then, the brass found out and nearly court-martialed me. My C.O. went to bat for me and saved me, but I had to go back to ground pounding."

"That seems so unfair," said Burt.

"That's what I thought too, and then came the final straw. I received a letter from Doc Brown. He was grief stricken to tell me, but Molly had died from the flu. She had been faithfully waiting my return when she would have been 20," he trailed off.

"We lost family, too," said Burt. "Nearly every family lost one or two. You must have been heartbroken."

"I was more than that, I was suicidal. I'd seen so much death; now one more."

"I can see why you don't want to bring up those memories," sympathized Burt, "but there's nothing dangerous about feeling grief or even thinking of suicide — we've all had those feelings. You don't have to tell me more, I'll understand."

"But I need to tell, especially to you," he confessed. "I was sent back to the rear with a wagon load of wounded. In the staging area, I met a French nurse who agreed to take me to her family home."

"You deserted the Army?" said a surprised Burt.

"Yes. I managed to bounce around France for two years. I lived with several families in the south of France where there wasn't much Allied presence. I worked in a French restaurant and even managed to learn enough French to fool the border guards. I went to Italy for a few months. When I came back across the border, they discovered my forged passport and deported me."

"So you've been bouncing around ever since? Are you still considered a deserter?" Burt queried.

"Now comes the part I'm not too proud of. I spent a year in the Federal Pen for desertion and forgery. While in the big house, I was a cook and sometimes a doc. I met some powerful people who were in the smuggling business. When I got out, I couldn't get a job, so I contacted those people. I became a rum runner from Canada to the cities in the Midwest. It was good money, a racy life and a bit dangerous, not as dangerous as life in the trenches though."

"So now you're out here in the wilds of Montana running from the law and the mob," Burt sighed.

"That life seems so distant now. I've finally found what I want and need — a family, a little farm and a good woman."

He got up off his log perch and walked behind Burt. He put his hands on her shoulders and massaged her neck. She shuddered and tingled, not trusting her feelings. She was about to stand up and face him when they heard voices coming up the trail. Dougan threw another log on the fire and sat down on his log.

All five men came in together laughing and joking.

"Dad gets the prize — he caught the littlest fish," joked Billy. "But we did catch quite a few."

"Enough for breakfast?" asked Dougan.

"Yes, and can we have huckleberry pancakes, too?" echoed Ralph. "Grandpa and Kyle picked a whole bunch."

"Did you have to fight off the bears?" Burt asked W.D. and Kyle.

"No, but you better appreciate every berry. It took us two hours to pick three quart bean cans full."

"What's up for tomorrow, Dad?" asked Billy.

"Well, there's a lot to do around here. I thought you and Ralph might like to ride down to Gooseberry Park where the three creeks come together to form Big River. That's where I want to go. We might even be able to catch a Dolly Varden trout," said Sandy with a tantalizing grin.

"That's for us!" said Ralph and Billy together.

"What else is there to do?" asked Ralph.

"You might want to climb Crystal Ridge," Sandy pointed in the direction of a hog's back ridge to the west. "You can find perfect quartz crystals lying right on the top of the ground. They are exposed by the wind and water erosion. Some folks have had them made into jewelry."

"How far is it?" asked Dougan.

"You should be able to get there and back in four hours plus whatever time you spend hunting for crystals," explained Sandy.

"Then, there's Johnny Sabado's cabin and corrals. Johnny is up here tending the cattle for several ranches that have grazing permits. He's pretty lonesome and will talk your leg off. He's a little different, but he would give you the shirt off his back."

W.D. spoke up. "I haven't seen Johnny for years. Kyle, let's drop in on him for lunch. He usually has something cooking in his stew pot."

"What do you want to do, Burt?" asked Sandy. "You're welcome to go fishing with us or visit Johnny. Or, we could climb Crystal Ridge either tomorrow evening or the next day."

"I think I'll just hang here in camp," she said. "I've got my book and maybe I can clean up a little. Five days of trail dust, horse sweat, campfires and in the same clothes is a little more than this lady can tolerate."

"Dougan, you could check the line fence up at the divide and fix any weak or broken spots. Then, you could explore Crystal Ridge if there's time. We'll probably be back by dinnertime," Sandy said as more of an order than a suggestion.

They watched the deer come out of the forest to browse in the meadow as the twilight rimmed the valley. Wisps of mist drifted along the creek bottom and a few bats fluttered and darted in the waning light. W.D. pulled out a cigar and Sandy filled and tamped his pipe.

"Dad, tell us about Dolly Varden trout," begged Billy. "Will we catch one tomorrow? What is the biggest one you've ever caught?"

"One question at a time, son. I know you're excited. Yes, we probably will catch one tomorrow, and my biggest Dolly was about 10 pounds. Grandpa can verify that."

W.D. blew a smoke ring toward the fire and then twirled the cigar in his fingers. "That was quite a fish. Your Dad caught it when he was 12, just like you. It happened in '02 when we had just moved to the Spring Hill Ranch. We borrowed horses from Frenchy Robert and came in the South

Fork to Gooseberry Park. Sandy tied a lure right to his fly line and threw it into a deep pool. That big fish practically chased Sandy out of the river as he attacked the lure. Sandy raced up and down the river bank screaming and hollering at every run. Finally, he beached the tired fish and we all stood around admiring its beautiful colors of yellow and red spots on a green background, silver flanks with more red spots."

"Did you eat it?" asked Billy.

"It fed the whole camp for two days," recalled W.D.

"Where do they come from, Grandpa?"

"They say they come up river from Flathead Lake where they live most of the year. Spawning season is July through September, so that's why they're in the upper reaches of Big River now."

"How did they get their name, Dolly Varden? That seems like a strange name for a fish."

"I can answer that," interrupted Burt. "Dolly Varden was a colorful character in one of Dickens' novels, *Burnaby Ridge*. Dolly was a society lady who wore outlandishly colorful dresses and hats. She inspired a whole fashion fad in the 1870s — wildly colorful petticoats covered with very thin skirts that had colorful patches and embroidery sewn in. Several of the rich town ladies had Dolly Varden dresses back in Delhi, Iowa, where I grew up."

"So how did that become a fish?" asked Billy.

"The fish looked so colorful; it was like a Dolly Varden dress to the wife of a Pacific Northwest angler. It was written up in the newspaper and the name stuck."

"So what is its real name?" asked Ralph.

Grandpa said, "We used to call them calico trout, but their real name is bull trout."

"I'd rather fight a bull than a dolly," quipped Billy.

The fire was down to embers when the group stumbled through the darkness to their bedrolls. There was a sliver of a moon, but the dim light didn't show the rocks and roots. Finally, the night was silent except for the tinkling horse bells in the distance. Sandy reached out and touched Burt in the darkness. "I'm ready tonight," he whispered.

Burt reached over and stroked his five-day growth of beard. "I'm afraid I'm a little too saddle sore. Maybe tomorrow when we've had a chance to clean up and rest up."

Sandy rolled over and soon was softly snoring. Burt lay awake, flooded with thoughts. Why had Dougan confessed? This was going to pose a big problem. What was she to do now that he had unburdened himself on her? Was she to feel sorry for him — feel attracted to him because he had made himself vulnerable — or feel obligated to comfort and "fix" him? She had rationalized that she could have a brief affair, share a little romance, and then he would move on. Now, things were different. He wanted more. This would be a turning point in her life. The repercussions could be tragic. Was her fulfillment worth it?

And then there was Sandy. She was beginning to really feel their age difference. He was 36 and she 46. She would soon be "change of life." She would be an old woman and he still a vibrant young man. Was he already feeling the difference? Was this part of his unromantic attitude, taking her for granted, and lack of sexual interest? She still had a good figure and was attractive to at least some men.

Mid life crisis — that's what they call it. I need adventure and romance in my life. Do I deserve it? Is it worth it? I could go live with my spinster sister in Los Angeles if I had to leave the T-6. I could take Betty and Beryl. Billy would insist on staying with his Dad. That would be the hardest part — the children. Tears welled up and spilled over onto her pillow which was a sack containing her day clothes. What a cruel twist, just as she had resigned herself to a lifetime of boring, isolated hard work as a ranch wife.

A coyote cried in the distance. The mournful sound seemed in sympathy to her soul. She thought of the lines of the old folk song:

If I had the wings of a turtle dove
Over these prison walls I would fly
I'd fly to the arms of my handsome one
And there I would live till I die.

Chapter XIV

Billy awakened at first light. It must be 4:00 A.M., he reasoned. He could see his breath in the morning air and could see some frost crystals on the nearby grass. He was cozy in his sleeping bag, but all he could think of was that big Dolly Varden trout in Big River. He had slept in his clothes with his boots for a pillow. He was dry and warm. He quickly pulled on his boots and made his way to the fire. He was surprised to see his Mom sitting by the fire. She had already kindled it back to life and was staring into the flames. "Mom, what are you doing up so early?"

"I couldn't sleep and I was getting cold," she replied. "I was thinking about you and your sisters."

"I wonder what Beryl and Betty are doing," Billy pondered. "I bet they're sleeping in and then having strawberries and cream for breakfast. Then, Grandma will have them do their needlework before they have fancy little sandwiches and tea for lunch."

"At this point, that sounds pretty good to me. Billy, have you ever thought what you'd do without me?"

"Mom, why would you say something like that? Are you sick or something?"

"No, Billy, I'm okay, but nothing in life is certain."

"You mean like Pastor Grant says, we have to be ready to go to heaven anytime because all of our days are numbered?"

"Something like that," sighed Burt.

"Mom, I couldn't live without you. Who would teach me

about the states and capitals; who would tuck me in and recite poetry about faraway places, who would help me find dragons and castles in the clouds?"

"Billy, you're almost a man now. You'll be finding your own dragons and castles. I love you with all my heart and I'm glad you treasure those memories."

"Maybe you could write a poem about the Dolly Varden trout I'm going to catch today!" said Billy encouragingly.

"I'll try, but I've got a lot on my mind."

The rest of the camp was stirring. "Is the coffee ready yet?" called Sandy.

"I'll put it on," replied Billy.

"You better go catch Pedro and four more saddle horses. We've got some fishing to do today."

Billy grabbed a handful of oats and a lead rope and walked to the meadow. The dew laden grass soaked his jeans and feet. He whistled and then listened for the horse bells. Finally, he saw a white animal at the far edge of the meadow. It must have been a mile, but Pedro started trotting toward Billy. When they met, Pedro nearly took Billy's jacket off trying to get the oats out of the pocket. "We make a good team, ol' boy," Billy said as he patted Pedro's neck and fed him the oats in his hand. Pedro's velvety lips tickled Billy's hand and then the long tongue cleaned up the last crumbs. Billy tied the lead rope to the halter and leaped onto Pedro's back. "Find the others, big fella." The other horses were grazing in a clearing out of sight from the meadow. Billy was able to catch four saddle horses and lead them all back to camp. Billy tied up the horses and walked into camp hungry enough to eat a bear.

"Hey, Billy, you're just in time for huckleberry pancakes. We've also got some huckleberry syrup. Ralph fried up the little trout, so we've got a real breakfast feast," said Dougan.

"I'll need some huckleberry power to pull in that big Dolly," Billy said as he gestured pulling in that big fish.

The pancakes and syrup were savored to the last bite. "You boys better go pick some more. This meal bears a repeat," complimented Burt.

"Bears is right. We might have to wrestle the bears to pick them," added W.D. "I saw a lot of purple bear scat on the trail."

"One old bear to another," joked Sandy.

"You boys go saddle your horses and get your fishing gear together. I'll make some extra pancakes for your lunch," offered Dougan.

"Hey, Billy, could you saddle my horse?" asked Ralph. "I'd like to stay and practice flipping pancakes."

"Okay, but you have to eat any that land in the ashes!" exclaimed Billy.

Billy brought the saddled horses into camp and the lunches, fishing gear and gifts for Johnny Sabados were loaded. Dougan put his fencing tools in a knapsack and started back toward the divide on foot. Sandy, Ralph and Billy mounted for Big River while W.D. and Kyle headed for the Sabados cabin.

"You boys have a good time," called Burt.

"You can come along and catch a big fish. This may be your last chance!" called Billy.

"I'll be fine here cleaning up after you messy men," quipped Burt.

The fishermen followed Gateway Creek to Gateway Gorge. There, huge dome-like mountains formed a slot for the creek. It looked like a giant gate with pillars 1000 feet high on each side. The top of the north pillar connected to Crystal Ridge and the south pillar formed a divide with the Bowl Creek drainage. Billy dreamed he was going through the Straits of Gibraltar to a faraway land.

The trail crossed a rockslide strewn with huge boulders the size of horses. It jogged this way and that to navigate the moraine. They could hear water rushing in the distance and then came upon Gateway Falls. The falls spilled about 30 feet into a small pool and then cascaded down a boulder strewn causeway.

"This is as far as the Dollies can migrate upstream," yelled Sandy above the roar. "We'll go down to Gooseberry Park past the junction of all the creeks that form Big River to fish."

The trail leveled out and the creek grew in size as smaller tributaries contributed their trickles to the Pacific-bound flow. Billy was getting buck fever or bull trout fever as they trotted along. Soon, they came to a wide opening in the forest. Numerous camp sites for hunting and fishing surrounded the central opening.

"This must be a popular place," commented Ralph, "and it must be 30 miles from the nearest road."

No other campers were in sight as they came upon the banks of Big River. The river was 30 to 40 feet wide and could only be crossed at a few places. Billy could see fish in the crystal clear water.

"Are those Dollies?" he asked.

"No, son. Those are just the native cutthroat. You'll know it when you see a Dolly," replied Sandy.

They tied up their horses in the shade and loosened the cinches. They gathered their fishing tackle and lunches and headed for the river.

"Why do they call it Big River?" asked Ralph.

Sandy related, "It's derived from the Indian name which means big water. This is actually the middle fork of the Flathead River that eventually runs into Flathead Lake."

They put together their poles, strung the line and tied on flies. They waded into the river and started casting. "This water is cold, but not as cold as the Teton," remarked Ralph.

"Let's give a prize for the biggest fish, the smallest fish and the most fish," exclaimed Billy.

"How about the first fish?" yelled Sandy as he hooked a nice cutthroat.

They worked their way down stream catching several fish and releasing anything shorter than 12 inches. A large, deep pond formed against the far bank. As they looked into the pool, Billy's heart raced when a large dark form moved in the current. "What's that?" he whispered to his Dad.

"Now that's a big Dolly Varden trout, son!"

Billy quivered as he cast his fly in front of the monster. As it drifted past, several small cutthroat tried to take the fly. Cast after cast did not interest the fish. "You'll have to try a bigger lure," suggested Sandy.

"I left them in the saddle bag. I'll go get one," said Billy as he was already running toward the horses.

"We should just as well go with him and eat lunch," said Ralph.

Billy frantically emptied the saddle bags. Only a pair of gloves, some twine and wire and the huckleberry pancakes fell out. He searched the other bags and found no other fishing tackle.

"I must have grabbed the wrong saddle bag," lamented Billy. "Now what can we do to catch that big Dolly?"

"Let's eat and think about it," said Sandy. "Maybe the bags got switched and went with Grandpa and Kyle."

"Or maybe Dougan thought they were the fencing tools, or maybe they're still in camp," pondered Billy.

They built a fire and roasted their trout on sticks over the coals. Huckleberry pancake trout sandwiches.

"Does lunch get any better than this?" Ralph asked.

Billy and his Dad discussed the options: Ride back to camp and get the lures, come back tomorrow and hope the fish would still be there or forget about that fish and continue catching the fat cutthroat residents of the river.

Billy decided to go back for the lures. Dad and Ralph would stay and fish. It was noon. Billy should be back by 2:00 and then they all could start back about 5:00 for dinner at 6:00, hopefully with a huge Dolly Varden trout lashed to the back of the saddle. He coaxed Pedro into a trot and backtracked toward Big River Meadows.

Dougan threw the fencing tools in a knapsack and headed back toward the divide. The trail was dusty even though it had rained only two nights ago. Hundreds of years of game, horse and people traffic had worn the trail a foot deeper than the surrounding meadow. Dougan could see the tracks of bear, wolf, deer, elk and shod horses. He was beginning to be a real mountain man. He liked the idea. Maybe it was time to stop running and settle down. His past shouldn't catch up with him here. He thought about what it would be like to be a rancher like Sandy. Nowadays, with homesteading over, it would be nearly impossible to get the capital together to start a ranch. He had no money and no cattle baron father.

He got to the fence line. The gate was tight and there were no horse tracks on the other side of the fence. He walked the line for about 100 feet. He pounded in a couple of staples and sat down on a log. The day was getting hotter and he could smell the pitch of the forest. He could also smell huckleberries. That meant bears could be nearby, a thought that made him cautious. He whistled and talked out loud as he walked the line.

What was Burt doing back at camp? She was there alone. Maybe he could fake the fencing repair and go back to camp. He thought of her constantly. She was not like any of the other women in his world. She was smart yet naïve, adventurous yet cautious, maiden-like yet matronly. Was he looking for the mother he wished he had? The urge overcame him. He started back down the trail to camp.

॥

Burt relished her respite from the man's world of camp life. She puttered about straightening up the camp site and picked a bouquet of wildflowers. The sun was above all the trees and mountain tops so the meadow was in full light. It was going to be a warm day, a perfect setting for reading her book, bathing in the creek and daydreaming. She was browsing through her Longfellow volume and came to the *Song of Hiawatha*. She yearned to be swept off into the sunset with no need to make hard choices, no need to be practical or calculating — just to live for the moment. She envied the eagle circling high above the cliff face. From that vantage, it could see all the possibilities; to kill, to mate, or to float on the currents. If only it were that simple.

After four days on the trail, she was ready for a bath. She contemplated heating water on the fire and taking a sponge bath. Somehow, that didn't seem adequate, so she would bathe in the creek. She hadn't done that since she went dipping with her sisters back in Iowa. They snuck away to the swimming hole. They suspected that the local boys might show up. They secretly hoped the boys would show up as they strutted their young bodies. She sang the little rhyme her sisters had sung:

Once I went in swimmin'
Where there were no women
Down by the deep blue sea.
Seeing no one there,
I hung my underwear
Upon a willow tree.
Then I dove into the water
Just like Pharaoh's daughter
In the Nile.
Someone saw me there

And stole my underwear
And left me with a smile.

She found a bar of soap and a towel and set off for the creek. The main creek was about 200 yards from camp. It meandered through willow clumps and brushy thickets. She was careful not to walk through thistle or stinging nettle patches. The creek bank was steep and a bit slippery and led to a gravel bar that jutted out into the stream. Burt watched the small trout rising for insects and darting back for the cover of the over-hanging bank on the far side. She judged the water to be about waist deep at the deepest.

She sat on a large flat rock and proceeded to get undressed. This was no small task. First, came the riding boots and then, the trousers. After nearly a week wearing pants she was still awkward at getting them on and off. Then, off with the shirt. She was standing there in her corset, long hose and hat. "I'll bet the bears get a laugh out of this outfit," she chuckled to herself. She unclamped her garters and peeled off the long hose. She was glad she decided to wear the stockings under her pants. The extra layer really cut down on the chafing from the saddle. Next, came the corset. She had been wearing a corset since she was a teenager. All the "proper" girls wore one. The size had changed a bit since then, but the overall shape was still the same. It did a good job of holding up her hose, holding in her stomach, but most importantly, supporting her rather generous breasts. She was glad she had the good support on a trotting or galloping horse. Billy called her corset her suit of armor. Hugging her in her armor was like hugging a statue. He liked hugs when she was in her nightgown. Finally, she undid her hair. The hat she had been wearing had smashed out all her finger waves. She fluffed them out and let her hair fall all around her face. She felt free and wanted to dance, but the rocky gravel bar was hard on her tender feet.

Then, she stepped in the water. "Oh, oh," she gasped as the cold water rose to her ankles. Gradually, she worked her way to the middle of the pool. The water was just above her waist. She braced herself as she splashed water on her chest and arms. Then, she put her face and head into the water. She was lathering her body when she had the feeling she was being watched. She reflexively covered her breasts and sank into the chilly water.

"You really have a beautiful body that you try to cover up with all that paraphernalia," said a voice from the opposite bank. "You look like a Maxfield Parrish nymph."

Then she saw him. Dougan had his shirt off and was sloshing into the creek toward her. She turned her back to him and kept covered. When he reached her, he gently touched her shoulder and turned her toward him. In a moment, they were embracing. He held her close and then kissed her on her neck and between her breasts. The cold water seemed hot as he stroked her breasts and gently squeezed her rock hard nipples. "Oh, Jack, take me away," she whispered.

Billy rode into camp from the back through the timber. It was a shortcut. The camp was deserted. He went to the tack pile and rummaged through the saddlebags that were left — no fishing tackle. "Did Grandpa accidentally take the saddle bags with the tackle he asked himself?" He went to the bedrolls. No tackle there. He was disappointed and even frustrated. He thought he might be able to make a lure out of a piece of silverware or tin can. He looked for the tool bag, but remembered Dougan had taken it fencing. He was about to cry when he heard a big splash at the creek and then laughter. It sounded like Mom.

He ran down to the creek just as Dougan came over the

bank carrying Burt. Burt was naked and wet. She still had soap in her hair. Dougan was shirtless and all wet, too. When they saw Billy, Burt cried, "Put me down, Dougan."

Billy stood there staring at his mother. He had never seen her completely naked before.

"It's not what you think, Billy," Burt said guiltily. "I was taking a bath in the creek and slipped and fell. Dougan helped me out."

Dougan had brought Burt's clothes from the gravel bar. "Turn your backs boys while I get dressed," ordered Burt.

Billy turned and ran back to camp and Pedro. He forgot about the fishing lure and tried to make sense out of what he had just witnessed. All he could think of were the cows in heat and the bulls fighting to breed. What was Dougan doing there? He was supposed to be off building fence. What was Mom doing there? Did they breed in the water? Was he taking her away to a bed or did she really fall and he rescued her? It didn't add up. He didn't want to wait in camp. It was only two o'clock. He jumped on Pedro and headed back to Gooseberry Park.

Billy didn't notice the rockslide, the waterfall or the towering pillars of Gateway Gorge. His mind was flooded by questions he wasn't sure he wanted answers for. Was Mom telling the truth? What was Dougan doing there? Should he tell Dad? Pedro was galloping down the trail as if he sensed the urgency of the situation. Billy was getting more anxious and angrier each mile. He liked Dougan. After all, he had saved the last royal coachman. But how dare he take advantage of Mom. The thought brought a big lump in his throat. And what about Mom, had she encouraged this somehow?

He thundered into Gooseberry Park and up to the tie-up rail. Pedro was lathered with sweat, but settled down quickly as he stood next to Punch and Judy. Billy called "Dad, Ralph."

He ran to the river bank and found them cleaning a nice mess of fish.

"You got back in a hurry. That big fish is still there; go catch 'em, Billy," greeted Ralph.

"I didn't find the lures," blurted Billy, "and there's something else." Billy looked anxious and agitated.

"What else? Is something wrong? Is Pedro hurt? Did a bear get into camp? What, Billy?"

"Dad, there's a problem. I have to talk to you."

Chapter XV

Burt cradled her head in her hands as she sat on a log back in camp. She thought of the tragic operas in which the frustrated lovers committed suicide or were killed by the vengeful third party. She wondered what Billy might be feeling and what he might say. Her chest ached and her eyes burned. What had she done?

Dougan walked up behind her and reached out to touch her shoulder. "Don't touch me!" she snarled. "We're in enough trouble already. How could I have been so stupid?"

"We don't need to make excuses for being in love. We were meant to be. There's no power greater than that. Remember, *"truth is beauty, beauty truth. That is all we know and all we need to know."* *

"It isn't that simple. A vagabond like you has nothing to lose. I have everything to lose: family, home, reputation." She was sobbing.

"What's your life worth? Don't let it slip away."

"That's what I would be doing. Throwing my present life away; for what, a few years of romantic uncertainty? Jack, I'm 46."

"Right, and you might be dead in 10 years, and what would you have missed?"

"I can't sacrifice my children on a romantic whim. They need me and I need them. I'm sorry," she said.

---

* *Ode to a Grecian Urn,* John Keats

"We'll have to find a way. I'm not giving up that easily."

They heard horses snorting and nickering, then, voices coming from the tie up area. Wolf and Patch came galloping past heading for the meadow. They stopped at the edge and rolled in the dirt, Wolf going completely over two times.

"One hundred dollars for every time he goes all the way over," said W.D. "I'll buy him."

"Sandy might have something to say about that," returned Kyle.

Burt stood up. "Don't say anything," she whispered to Dougan. "I'll do the talking."

W.D. and Kyle strolled into camp.

"You boys are back early. How's Johnny?" asked Burt.

"I hope we're not interrupting anything here," said W.D. in an accusing tone. "Johnny's fine. He was glad for some company and some groceries. He would rather have had a bottle, but that would be against the law. Isn't that right, Dougan?"

Dougan nodded and began working on dinner. He knew where that discussion might lead.

Burt stepped in. "I'm going to wash up for dinner and maybe get a little nap. Those huckleberries are all gone — do you suppose you could find some more?"

Kyle and W.D reckoned they could go wrestle the bears for a few more berries. W.D. has his .45 on his hip.

Billy walked away from the river back to where the horses were tied. His heart galloped in his chest and his face felt like it was on fire. His Dad followed dreading what was about to be announced. Billy rehearsed the scene. He was still angry and wanted to get back at Dougan. He really didn't consider his mother at that point.

"Dad, I've got to tell you what happened back at camp," he said breathlessly.

"Calm down, son. Talk it slow and easy."

"Dad, he and Mom were naked down by the creek, at least Mom was naked. And he was carrying her."

"Who, Billy, who?"

"Dougan. He was like a bull with a cow in heat."

Sandy gulped and sat down on a log. "Tell me again, slower this time."

"I heard them laughing and splashing down in the creek. I went down there and found Dougan carrying Mom. When they saw me, she said "Put me down." Then, he got her clothes and she got dressed. I ran back to camp and then came here."

"Did Mom say anything?"

"She said, "It's not what you think, Billy.""

Sandy sat in silence for several minutes. Billy watched as he drummed his fingers on a log and then got out a cigarette and lit it. Billy knew better than to interrupt those churning thoughts.

"I think I better go back. You and Ralph stay here for a while. Maybe you can catch a few more fish. Be careful." Sandy's voice was quivering and measured as he put his hand on Billy's shoulder. "Don't worry, we'll figure this out."

Sandy mounted Punch and started up the trail at a trot. Billy watched him disappear into the timber. Billy's urge was to follow and find out what Dad would do. Dad could fix anything and figure out anything.

His throat was dry as a dust devil, his face flushed and tears streaked, and his heart was still throbbing like the Delco engine. He put his whole face into the river as he drank. The cool water felt so good as it washed away his tears and troubles. He drank deeply and finally came up to breathe.

"Were you looking for fish? I thought you'd never come up," called Ralph. "What's happening; where did your Dad go?"

W. David Jones 157

Billy hesitated on how much to tell Ralph. He even wondered if he should have told his Dad the details. "Dad had to go back to camp to settle something with Dougan. We need to be back in time for dinner."

"Then we have time to catch a few more fish. We'll have a real feast." Ralph was already building his loop and laid a perfect cast some 30 feet to a rising cut.

Sandy double checked his Winchester in the scabbard. Five rounds in the magazine, chamber empty. He rehearsed every possible scene as Punch walked up the canyon trail on auto pilot. He had noticed flirting going on between them, but Burt was known to do that among the men of the community. She could coax even that curmudgeon Shorty Cornet into giving a dollar to the Ladies Aide.

Who should he confront first, Dougan or Burt? It would be unlikely they would be together, and if they were, it probably meant they were guilty.

Burt was witty and decisive. She could put down a student twice her size with a word or even a gesture. She would have been able to put down Dougan if she had wanted to. She may have even encouraged the advance. Dougan was a worldly man and probably had had many women in this past. He knew all the right moves, certainly more than a Montana country boy.

And what of his own relationship with Burt? In the beginning, it had been exciting and intense. They worked together building their new big house. They made love in every room or whenever the wind blew. The result of that was Billy one year later and Beryl three years later. They worked hard to build the ranch and family. Sex became infrequent after Beryl. Burt didn't want any more children. He had sent off for some French skins, but somehow sex wasn't the same. He could see her becoming an old woman. Their roles seemed to change, she wanting to be involved in ranching and he resenting her interference in the development of his ranch. They had frequent arguments over their roles.

W.D. had warned him about marrying an older woman, but that was her main attraction. She was strong, independent, smart and very attractive to him. She had so much more to offer than the girls his own age. W.D. had never really embraced her as a daughter-in-law. They seemed to have a standoff relationship from the start.

So who was to blame? Dougan who took advantage of a frustrated housewife, W.D. who openly showed his dislike for Burt, Burt who was headstrong and refused to be the submissive wife, or himself who had neglected to romance his wife and had taken her for granted?

In any event, this was going to be an unpleasant and possibly dangerous end to what had started out as a pleasant day.

He was startled by the roar of the falls and he listened hoping he could hear an answer in the chattering cascade. What would his Dad do in this situation? He remembered the night 25 years ago when W.D. led a posse hunting down a pair of horse thieves. When the posse found the thieves hiding in a coulee along with the stolen horses, they hung the pair on the spot. "Shoot first and ask questions later," was one of his frequent sayings. The old code sometimes allowed shooting a wife stealer.

Dougan was a drifter — who would miss him? He could have an unfortunate accident and disappear out here in the wilderness. But what if he was wrong? Were Burt and Dougan guilty? Of course, they would lie at gun point.

The horse stumbled on a loose rock and Sandy was jolted to the present. Camp was only minutes away. He had to have a plan. A stone came bouncing down the slide and ricocheted over his head. I wonder who threw that stone, he thought. A phrase struck him as if the stone had hit him. "Let he who is without sin cast the first stone." He remembered the Bible story of Jesus and the woman who had been caught in adultery. According to Jewish law, the woman was to be stoned to death, but Jesus told the officials and the crowd, "Let he who is without sin cast the first stone." No one threw a stone and the crowd dispersed. Jesus then said to the woman, "I do not condemn you. Go and sin no more" (John 8:1-11).

Punch heard the other horses and whinnied out to them. Sandy knew his entrance had been announced. He tied up and unsaddled Punch. He pulled the rifle from the scabbard and strode into camp. Burt was sitting on a log pretending to read a book. Dougan was gone. A long moment of icy silence was broken by a crash in the brush across camp. Sandy raised his rifle as Dougan came into camp dragging a dead tree for firewood.

Dougan yelled across the clearing, "Hey, boss, you're back early. Did you catch a big fish?"

Burt shot Dougan a withering glance and put her finger to her lips.

Sandy stepped toward Dougan, rifle at the ready. "Yeah, I'm back early. I've got some business to tend to, you son of a bitch."

Burt stood up and walked toward Sandy. "Billy must have told you what he saw. Sandy, believe me, that's all there was to it."

"Why should I believe you? It's too convenient for all this to happen when you knew camp would be empty. I always wondered why you came along on the trip. Now, I know why."

"Please, Sandy, let's talk this out. There's an explanation." Don't do anything rash," pleaded Burt.

"Who's talking about doing something rash? I could shoot the both of you and probably get away with it."

"This is 1927, not 1887. You would go off to prison and leave three orphans. Think about it," reasoned Burt.

Sandy lowered the rifle and then looked at Dougan. "I was beginning to like and trust you. I thought you were a cut above the average cow hand, but you're just an opportunistic drifter. I'll bet there's a warrant out for you. You're in my sights. I might get a bounty for shooting you, you whore-mongering bastard. Damn you to hell!"

Dougan slowly retreated to the far side of the fire pit and started laying kindling for evening cooking. Nothing was said as Burt and Sandy watched the ritual. Sandy was white and trembling with anger. Burt knew enough to be silent. She had never heard Sandy curse at anyone or anything.

The silence was broken by voices coming down the trail. W.D. and Kyle entered the camp. They saw the trio frozen in position: Sandy with his rifle across his chest, Dougan squatted by the fire and Burt sitting on a log, her book at her feet.

"What's going on?" interrupted W.D.

"Dougan and Burt are getting ready to pack up and leave," choked out Sandy.

"Why? What happened?" asked W.D.

"We've got some business to settle. It's personal," said Sandy.

Burt jumped to her feet. "Now don't you men get any ideas like a lynching mob. You don't know the facts."

"Then let's hear them," said W.D.

"Just my husband and me. Then, it's up to my husband," she calmly replied. She emphasized the word husband.

"I think we all better leave. Get the horses together. We'll head out at daylight," said Sandy.

"What about supper tonight?" said Dougan.

"We'll manage. The boys have a big mess of fish and we can eat up a few cans of beans. Get out of here and round up the horses," ordered Sandy.

Back at Big River, Billy couldn't concentrate on fishing. He missed the strike on several fish. Ralph already had four and had released several small ones. Billy waded toward Ralph only to slip on a rolling rock and fall headlong into the cold water.

"What's the matter, Billy? You're acting like a real dud?" quipped Ralph.

Billy was soaking wet and angry and everything. He whipped his pole at Ralph, catching him across the legs.

"Easy cousin, I was only teasing. I know you're upset. Tell me what happened."

Billy was on the verge of tears. He backed out of the river and found a sunny rock to sit on to warm up and dry out. His emotions were churning. He was embarrassed for whipping Ralph, angry at Dougan and his mother and fearful for his father. What had he started? Was he a tattletale? What should he tell Ralph? The warm August sun quickly dried out his clothes and calmed his angst. He began rehearsing a revision in the story he had told Dad. He would say he saw Mom fall in the creek and Dougan came to her rescue. He hoped the new version would fix everything.

Ralph came up from the river with his four fish. "Are you done fishing, Billy? I'm sorry I teased you. Come help me clean the fish."

"I'm sorry I whipped you. I don't know why I did it. I was mad and embarrassed. You were just the first thing I saw. I wanted to hit someone. I guess you were a substitute or a scapegoat," blurted Billy.

"Who did you want to hit?"

Billy quickly realized that he shouldn't tell Ralph the details. He tried to think of an alternative. "I guess myself for forgetting the Dolly Varden lures."

"Whatever you say," replied Ralph, "but I do forgive you. Now, let's clean the fish."

As Billy slit the belly of a big trout, he wondered what it

would feel like to slit a man's belly. The thought repulsed him as he teased out the entrails and scooped out the blood line and kidneys of tonight's supper.

They gathered the day's catch, some 20 trout, and wrapped them in wet leaves and burlap. Then, they tied the bundle behind the saddle.

"We'll need to re-wet the wrap frequently to keep them cold," said Billy. "Let's start back. We'll get there in plenty of time for supper."

They put away the fishing tackle and mounted up. Pedro strained to eat the hillside grass. Billy realized that he hadn't allowed Pedro to graze or even drink since morning.

"Sorry, old boy. I can't do anything right today."

The trail back to the meadows looked different even though Billy was retracing it for the fourth time today. At the first stream crossing, Pedro drank steadily for five minutes. Billy got off and splashed some water on the trout.

"Why did your Dad leave? Is something wrong back at camp?" pumped Ralph.

"I can't tell," screamed Billy angrily. "Just mind your own business."

"Easy, cousin. I'm not the bad guy. I won't mention it again."

Pedro paced off the mile toward camp dodging the rocks and catching a mouthful of tall grass or thistle tops as they passed by. Soon, they were in the corral area and noticed the whole herd of horses there and tied up. Billy dismounted and unsaddled Pedro who immediately laid down and rolled over three times.

"You better get a bite to eat, big fella. It looks like we might be moving."

Billy and Ralph walked into camp with their sack of fish. Nobody greeted them or asked them where the big fish was. Finally, Sandy said, "You better get at cooking those fish. That's what for dinner."

"Just fish? Nothing else?" questioned Ralph.

"The pantry box is yours. Use your imagination," said Sandy.

"Where's Dougan? He could make something fancy."

"He's got other duties."

"We could make huckleberry pancakes. I see someone picked more huckleberries," said Billy.

"That would be good," said Sandy, "and while you're at it, cook enough for breakfast and lunch tomorrow. We're leaving at dawn"

Billy and Ralph got out the griddle and the big cast iron fry pan. They spread out the coals in the fire and balanced the pans. Ralph mixed up the pancake batter while Billy floured the fish and melted the bacon grease in the big pan. The fish were so much bigger than this morning's minnows. They had to cut the heads and tails off most of them so they would fit in the pan, and then only five in a batch. Finally, they had all 20 fish cooked and a stack of at least 50 pancakes.

Burt was sitting silently at the far edge of the camp. She came up to the cooking area and admired the fish and cakes. "I need to talk to you, Billy. Please come to my spot after cleanup."

Billy nodded but didn't say anything. He wanted to yell, "Why did you do it, Mom?", but instead focused on the big stack of fish in the Dutch oven.

"Come and get it, or I'll throw it out!" yelled Ralph.

Everyone filed by and took a fish and a few pancakes. Most took a cup of side boiled coffee and then sat around the fire to eat.

Sandy cleared his throat and addressed the group.

"Something has come up and we have to go back. We're going to try to get all the way back to the car in one day. We need to start at dawn, so we'll have to pack up tonight. Breakfast will be leftover trout and pancakes. Put a few cakes in your saddle bags for lunch."

"But, Dad, it took us three days to get here; how can we get home in one day?"

"It will be a long, hard ride, but we can do it. I'm counting on you, son."

"But why, Dad? I didn't get to catch a Dolly Varden trout."

"Maybe next year. I think you know why we have to go home."

Everybody stared at Billy waiting for an explanation, but he just stared into the fire. Dougan offered to help with the dishes, but Sandy ordered him to pack up the supplies and carry them to the corral area, also to take down the rain fly tarp. "It's not going to rain tonight."

Ralph and Billy sacked up the leftover trout and pancakes and strung them up high on the bear wire. They then packed up the dishes and cooking equipment into the pack boxes.

"Save out the canned sardines and Vienna sausages for the trip out," ordered Sandy.

"Your Dad is a regular drill sergeant," commented Ralph. "What's got into him?"

"It's important that we get all the way out tomorrow. He means business," answered Billy.

It was nearly dark when Billy sought out his Mom. She was alone sitting on her bedroll. He knew she was embarrassed, hurting and, he hoped, sorry. He wanted to ask her a million questions, but didn't know how to start. He just stood there awkwardly. Finally, Burt spoke. "Sit down, Billy. I know you're confused and maybe angry. Please hear me out."

Billy cautiously sank to his haunches, ready to spring and run and waited for the impending lightning strike.

"Billy, I love you more than you can know and I'm so proud of you. You're almost a man. I couldn't have wished for a better son. I made a mistake and let my school girl fantasies cloud my judgment. Maybe when you're a little older, you'll understand more. I was flattered and tempted by Dougan, but trust me, nothing happened. Believe me! But no matter what happens, remember that I love you forever, and nothing can take that away."

Billy gulped and tried hard to hold back the tears. He wanted to hug his Mom and slap her at the same time.

He finally whispered, "I love you too, Mom," as he stood up and walked in to the brush.

Chapter XVI

It was still mostly dark when Sandy bounded around the camp shaking the forms under each bedroll. "Up'n at 'em, cowboys," he called to the crew. "Daylight is burning and we have miles to go."

Billy wondered if his Dad went to bed at all. He got up, rolled up his bed tucking his personal articles inside the roll. He would tie it on his saddle as the pack boxes were already wrapped up. Venus was bright in the early dawn sky hovering over Corrugated Ridge on the divide. He walked to the creek and splashed off before reeling in the food bag from the bear line. The others were up by now and grabbing a mouthful of cold fish and pancakes. Some made sandwiches of fish and pancakes for their saddle bags. Billy fixed himself a sandwich and made one for his mother.

Burt went down to the creek by herself. She had slept alone and was feeling shunned by the men. She couldn't muster any small talk or teasing to break the tension. She dreaded this day.

Dougan was down at the corral when Sandy arrived. He was dutifully putting on the pack saddles and the tie down lines. "Good morning, Mr. Jones. I imagine this is the last time I'll be doing this."

Sandy grunted and went to untie a pack horse to take to the camp site.

Dougan continued, "I know you're pissed at me and you have a right to be, but let me tell you, nothing happened between Burt and me. I had no business sneaking up on her or touching her, but she did fall down in the creek and I helped her out."

"You expect me to believe that from a world traveler, rum-runner, desperate drifter, con man now turned saint," scathed Sandy. "You better shut up and not dig yourself any deeper."

Dougan and Sandy led the pack horses to the pile of pan-yards ready to be loaded.

In only a few minutes, all the packs were loaded and cinched down. Each saddle bag had a share of the fish and pancakes plus a tin of sardines and a few sticks of candy. The saddled horses were ready and everyone mounted up just as the sun peeked over the eastern horizon. There wasn't a cloud in the sky. It promised to be a hot day.

"You know, you don't have to do this," Burt quietly said to Sandy through gritted teeth. "You don't have to be a Simon Legree."

"That's a good way to put it," said Sandy. "I'm evicting you from Paradise. We're leaving the Garden of Eden. The devil has shown his ugly head here and we're leaving temptation here at the meadows."

With determined set of his jaw, he yelled, "Move 'em out! Burt will ride behind me, Kyle and W.D. in the middle. Billy — take four pack horses and Dougan take five. Ralph, you ride with Billy."

"Yes, sir!" Dougan snapped sarcastically.

Billy looked back at Big River Meadows and wondered if he'd ever see it again or be back for that big Dolly Varden trout. He gave Pedro a little heel and stepped out at a brisk walk. He agonized over his part in this sudden exit. What if he hadn't told?

They crossed back over the Continental Divide and into the south fork of Birch Creek drainage. The sun was in their faces and the heat was building at only 8 A.M. At the first watering site, everybody dismounted and drank or relieved themselves. They didn't set up the screen for Burt, so she had to find a secluded bush. Sandy was barking out marching orders before she had even unbuttoned.

The two pack strings got to the ford just as the advance riders were leaving. Sandy told them to make time the best they could while he, Burt, W.D. and Kyle would go as fast as they could to the Blackleaf trailhead.

The horseflies were unusually numerous and aggressive. The horses were kicking their bellies and switching their tails incessantly. The flies were biting right through clothing and leaving welts or even oozing sores. Burt was developing a large welt on her jaw line and another on her hand. "Let's stop at the next shady spot and mud pack the bites," she pleaded.

"The bugs will be just as bad in the shade," returned Sandy, "besides, we don't have time. Maybe we can stop briefly for lunch."

Sandy set a furious pace down Birch Creek Canyon. Punch could pace at four to five miles per hour; unfortunately, the other horses couldn't walk that fast, so they broke into a bone jarring trot every few minutes to catch up. Burt was already a little saddle sore from the trip in. Now, she was really in misery. The trotting and downhill bouncing was not at all pleasurable today.

Sandy went past the Crazy Creek fork in the trail and on down Birch Creek. He turned back to W.D. and called, "Let's take Phone Creek back. The trail is not so steep and rocky."

"I think that's best, too. We don't need to disturb old Jacques La Fleur again. Maybe he has something to do with this situation," replied W.D.

Burt looked daggers at both men, but didn't say anything. She wondered how much W.D. knew. She feared the vigilante justice reputation. She could usually reason with Sandy, but not W.D.

It was 10:00 A.M. when the advance party reached the Phone Creek junction — twelve miles in four hours. Sandy was satisfied with that pace. It would be slower going uphill to Phone Creek Pass and, hopefully, the trail would be cleared. That trail was less used than Crazy Creek trail. A breeze had started out of the west and the flies were not so horrible. Burt was hurting, but thinking she could probably make it. At the headwaters of Phone Creek, they stopped for water and lunch. When they stopped, the flies caught up with them and had lunch too. The pancakes and fish sandwiches were dry, but the water was cold and sweet.

Remount time. Burt was so stiff and sore, she couldn't swing up and over. Sandy had to help. They started up the steep portion of Phone Creek pass. The switchbacks were tight and the horses were grunting with every step. Burt welcomed sitting back in the saddle and protecting her chafed and aching upper inner thighs. Then came another long downhill into Teton Canyon. As the horses slid stiff legged down the incline, Burt screamed in agony. "You might as well whip me and leave me to die on the trail. Is that what you're trying to do?"

Sandy gritted his teeth and returned, "We're making good time. You can sleep in your own bed tonight."

"You mean my own coffin, you slave driver."

Nobody noticed the rugged beauty of the pass. The west side of Mount Wright and Mount Frazier were totally different that the eastern front. Beautiful fingers of timber climbed up the draws. The area above the tree line was a smooth 45-degree incline right up to the peak where the cliff face dropped off to the east.

The north fork of the Teton River valley was wider and glaciated compared to Phone Creek. The trail was flat and straight. It cut through old growth timber and offered some shade from the sweltering sun. The forest smelled hot and pitchy. The flies were back and attacked ferociously so the horses danced, kicked and flicked their tails only to divert the flies to the humans. Even though it was hot, they all turned up their collars, rolled down their sleeves and put on scarves. They looked like a troop of outlaws.

When they forded the river, the horses stood in belly deep water to soothe the fly bites. Sandy made sure they all drank deeply. The next segment would be the toughest yet.

It was 3:00 o'clock when they left the Teton and started up Blackleaf Trail. The sign said Blackleaf eight miles. Burt remembered the arduous climb over Blackleaf Pass five days ago. She dreaded the steep climb, the tight switchbacks and the loose rocks on the trail. She could feel moisture on her inner thighs. She hoped it was only sweat and not weeping broken blisters.

"Are you hurt?" Sandy called back. "There's blood running down your face."

"As if you'd care!" returned Burt.

She reached up and felt the wet, sticky blood on her brow and cheek, then felt the welt rising from the fly bite. She must have splattered the fly as it sucked her blood.

"I do care about you. You're my wife and I still love you, believe it or not," Sandy said with sincerity. "Do you need a dressing or bandage on your head?"

"No, it's just another horsefly bite. I'll live."

The weary procession climbed the third pass of the day. The horses were stumbling and grunting. Sweat dripped from their chests and flanks. At the top, a stiff wind shot through the gap and helped cool them before the downhill slide. Burt dreaded another jarring descent and winced with each stop. Finally, they were following Blackleaf Creek, past the falls and to the trailhead. The Hupmobile was waiting, no worse for wear, but it did have cow slobber on the windows.

The four riders unsaddled and let their horses run free. The horses rolled in the dirt, but were too tired to even roll over once.

"They will be fine here until the pack trains arrive. If they do get away, they'll head for home," said Sandy.

It was 5:30 P.M. They would be home before dark.

Chapter XVII

The Hup bounced over the rocks and ruts and through the "jaws" of Blackleaf Canyon. Kyle got to open and close the gate. W.D. and Sandy were in the front and Kyle and Burt in the back. The three men all smoked "roll your owns" until the air in the car was blue. The dust outside was just as choking as the Hupmobile rolled down the skid road at a speedy 15 miles per hour. After a thousand bumps and jolts, they reached the graded county road. The dust was even thicker there, but they could now go 35 miles per hour.

Sandy and W.D. discussed the work to be done back at the ranch. Kyle and Burt were silent. Burt dreaded the hours ahead when she and Sandy would be alone and forced to confront the issue. She was nauseous from the ride, the smoke, and the anxiety she was feeling. When they reached Spring Hill ranch, she got out of the car and retched the last traces of fish pancake sandwich.

Grandma Lilly, Beryl and Betty ran out to greet them. "You're home early," they exclaimed. "Is everything all right? Where are Billy and Ralph?"

"We're okay. Billy and Ralph will be home tomorrow with the pack strings," said Sandy.

"Stay for dinner," said Lilly. "We've got lots left over and plenty more where that came from."

"No thanks," said Sandy. "Burt's not feeling well and we need to get home."

"Please, Daddy, can we stay for a few days?" said Beryl and

Betty. "We're going to have a party with Grandma. We've invited our friends and it will be so much fun."

Sandy glanced at an ashen faced Burt and then nodded. "That'll be fine. Have a good time. We'll see you in a couple of days."

Long shadows touched the big barn and house as they pulled into the T-6. There was a beautiful sunset over the mountains which both ignored. The house was hot and stuffy and they hurried to open doors and windows to air it out. "Can I fry you an egg or two?" asked Sandy.

Burt cringed at the thought of food. "I've got to lie down. I'm sore from ankle to ankle, chewed raw by the horseflies, nauseated from your smoking and driving, and not about to eat some greasy fried eggs!" She climbed the stairs to the bedroom. She ached for a hot bath, but didn't have the energy to heat the water. She was barely able to take off her dusty, sweaty clothes and collapse in bed.

Sandy built a fire in the kitchen stove, filled the reservoir with water and then cooked himself eggs and hash browns. He wandered to the barn and stared at the moon rising in the east. He was proud of his ranch, of all the things he had accomplished. He was proud of his family and all his possessions, but what was wrong? He heard a voice in his head saying, "Pride cometh before a fall." He wandered back to the house. He filled the claw foot bathtub with hot water from the stove and walked upstairs. Burt was in bed but not sleeping.

"I've filled the bathtub for you and made a pot of tea. Maybe a bath will make you feel better."

Burt wondered if it was worth the effort to get up and take a bath, but she ached, itched and crawled all over. She hadn't even washed her face or hands before crashing. She got up and limped to the waiting tub. Even in her dirty, exhausted state, she was embarrassed to disrobe in Sandy's presence. "I could use some privacy," she blurted.

Sandy retreated to the next room, but stayed ready to assist if she had difficulty getting into the tub. Burt managed to get in. The hot water initially stung, but soon soothed the chafed spots or fly bite welts.

"May I bring you some tea?" he said softly.

Burt sank down further into the hot, soapy water. "That would be nice; a little sugar, please."

Sandy brought her the tea and then pulled a chair beside the tub. "I used to enjoy watching you bathe. Remember when we tried to get into that tub together?"

Burt smiled when she thought of that awkward moment. It was her first pleasant thought of the day.

Sandy whispered, "I would wash your back. I'll bet there are spots you can't scratch or get to."

Without a word from her, he lathered up the cloth and gently washed her neck and shoulders. She leaned forward so he could get to the entire back. He continued, "Whatever happened back at the meadow, I forgive you. You're more important to me than the ranch or the barn or the machinery — more important than the livestock or the crops. You're the partner God gave me and I love you. Can you forgive me for taking you so for granted and paying more attention to the cows than to you?"

Burt relaxed and leaned back. She took his hand and placed it on her breast. She was aching for intimacy, even though her thighs were chafed and sore. "Get into this tub, you smelly old goat," she teased. "I've got some forgivin' to give you."

They laughed and splashed water all over the kitchen floor. Then they stood in front of the warm kitchen stove and dried each other off. They broke their embrace to climb upstairs to the bedroom. Burt confessed she was too sore all over to make love on the rug. They fell asleep in each other's arms totally exhausted.

The next day, Burt and Sandy drove around the ranch

checking the crops, the cattle and the weeds. The wheat was still a week or two from harvest. The weeds in the summer fallow were thick and knee high and the cows had nearly exhausted the grass in the pasture.

"We've had our time to play. Now there's work to do," said Sandy. "This is the time we've waited all year for." He plucked several heads of wheat and shelled them out in his hand. He chewed several kernels and gave a small handful to Burt. "Chew these and see how much moisture remains. Are they dry enough to keep and hard enough to make flour?"

Burt chewed the wheat and felt good about being asked to help make the harvest decisions.

"It's not ready yet, but we better get on Charlie McDonald's list for harvesting the wheat. His new combine will make short work of harvest," replied Burt.

"I'm going to move the tractors and disc plows to the west field. Would you shuttle me back and forth? Dougan should be home tonight and we can start plowing first thing tomorrow morning."

Burt agreed. "Maybe Billy and Ralph can move the cows to the east pasture when they get back."

"That's a good idea. I think they can handle the job. They're getting to be good cowboys."

Billy and Ralph held back and let Dougan take the lead. The pack horses were making good time now that their load was much lighter. They crossed the divide and started down the South Fork drainage. In only one hour, they were down to the falls and ready for a break. The horses drank deeply and waded into the water to discourage the flies.

"Damn those pesky flies. They actually take a bite out of you," complained Ralph.

"It's only nine o'clock and I'm bitten all over, right through my shirt," echoed Billy.

Dougan stood off by himself smoking a roll your own.

"What's gotten into him? He's not usually so standoffish," commented Ralph.

"He's got a lot of thinking to do," answered Billy.

"What about?"

Billy again withheld the answer and changed the subject. "Ready for a snack? Pancake fish rollups or a stick of candy?"

They each took out a stick of candy out of their saddlebags and mounted up. "About an hour to the Fork, I reckon," said Dougan, the first words he had said all morning.

At the Crazy Creek Fork, they noticed no tracks going that direction and an arrow drawn in the dusty trail. "They are taking the easy way home," said Billy. "I guess we should follow them."

The day was getting hotter and the flies were swarming. Billy reached down and slapped three in one crack on Pedro's shoulder. The other horses were kicking and switching their tails constantly.

"I hope old Hank doesn't decide to buck the pack off the next time he gets bit," said Billy as he tightened up the jerk line.

At the Phone Creek Fork, the tracks went to the right and Dougan followed. They crossed Birch Creek and again waded into the water for a drink and to splash off the dust, sweat and bloody fly bites.

"Let's eat at the next crossing," said Billy.

The fish pancake sandwiches were dry and tasteless but they had good cold water to wash them down. "I thought I would never get tired of trout or huckleberry pancakes, but these are pretty bad," sighed Ralph.

"Don't complain about the cooking unless you want to do it," Billy and Dougan said in unison. It was the first light moment of the day. They tightened up the cinches that had been loosened for the lunch break and resumed the climb up Phone Creek Pass. "We're about halfway to camp. No turning back," said Billy.

They crested the pass and headed down the North Fork of the Teton. As they passed the first night's campground, Ralph relived that big "cut" that broke his line. "Somehow the ones that got away are more memorable than the ones we caught," philosophized Ralph. "I'll remember that fish until the day I die."

Even though the horses were caked with sweat and hungry, they seemed to have new energy as they headed up Blackleaf Pass. Little rivulets of gravel cascaded down from the switchbacks above, but nobody paid any attention. The wildflowers, rock creatures and soaring eagles were likewise ignored. As they approached the trailhead, the shadows of the peaks behind them were cooling them. They heard horses ahead and soon the camp was in sight. There was a pile of saddles and gear at the cabin.

"It looks like they're long gone," said Dougan. "We better make camp while we've still got a little daylight.

The freed horses immediately went to eating and the cowboys ate cold beans and sardines before collapsing in their bedrolls.

Dougan, Billy and Ralph were up at first light. The boys rounded up the horses while Dougan made a fire and breakfast. He fried up the last of the bacon and made a big pot of oatmeal. "There is not much food left for a trail lunch, so eat a big breakfast. I hope we make it home by supper time."

The horses seemed to know it was time to head for the T-6 and were clustered by the gate. Billy and Ralph saddled up the herd and then came in for breakfast.

"You boys are getting to be mighty good wranglers. I'll hire you when I get my ranch," praised Dougan.

They used the last of the canned milk on the oats and kid coffee. "I'll be glad to have fresh milk and real bread again, not that this grub isn't excellent," said Ralph.

The pack boxes were much lighter and the empty saddles made the horses frisky. They were on the trail by 8:00 A.M.

As they came to the horn of Blackleaf Canyon, the wind picked up and hurled dust and small rocks at their backs. "At least this will keep the flies away," shouted Billy. The horses were almost running as the stinging rocks and dust whipped their rumps. In no time they were out of the canyon and into the rangeland.

"This wind will blow us home," yelled Ralph.

"We'll get there before dinner," shouted Billy.

The three riders and 13 horses in toe could ride abreast across the prairie. Gophers scurried out of their way and stood up to whistle a warning. Dougan pulled his slingshot out of his pocket and let fly at one of the varmints. It toppled over in its tracks.

That's amazing, thought Billy. I couldn't even do that with a rifle from horseback.

The party crossed Blackleaf Creek for the last time. It had dried up to a trickle and the herd of horses nearly drank it dry. "No more water until we get to the Olson's reservoir. It's about five or six mile and then only five more miles home," Billy announced with great authority.

"I'm going to make you foreman on my ranch," said Dougan.

Billy was suspicious of Dougan. What was he up to? Billy hadn't spoken to Dougan since the incident at Big River Meadows. He was angry at Dougan, angry at Mom, and angry at himself for triggering the whole mess. He wondered if Dad and Mom were still together. He wondered if Dad would fire Dougan when they got home. He wondered if his life would ever be the same gain.

He awoke from his thoughts as Pedro sidestepped a badger

hole and nearly dumped him. Ralph laughed, "Asleep in the saddle? Maybe we should tie you on."

Billy was embarrassed. He pulled on the jerk line and started the whole pack string into a trot. The horses were heading home, so there was no stopping them. The wind was still at their backs and the flies were gone. They watered at the Olson's reservoir and ate the last of the sardines and Vienna sausages.

"Lunch was sure better on the trip in than out," commented Dougan.

"I wonder what's for supper," Ralph replied. "I bet it will be delicious and plentiful."

Billy finally decided to say something to Dougan. "What are you gonna do when we get back?"

Dougan squirmed, "That's up to your Dad. I imagine he'll start harvest or fall tilling."

"Are you staying for harvest?"

"I told your Dad I'd stay through harvest, so it's up to him."

Billy didn't reply. He couldn't imagine his Dad letting Dougan off the hook. He wondered if Dad and Dougan had had it out. All of a sudden, he was dreading going home. How could be face Mom or Dad?

The last seven miles seemed to fly by. They crossed the burn, now greening up, the Sullivan ranch and soon they could see the big red barn glowing like a ruby in the afternoon sun. At three o'clock, they rode into the corral and tied up. Ralph pumped a trough of water for the horses and men. They unsaddled the horses and piled up the packs and saddles by the barn door.

The horses bolted for the pasture and had a good roll in the dust. The three men walked toward the house. Sandy came out to meet them. "Welcome back; you made good time. Supper will be at six. Maybe you would like to clean up or take a nap?"

Dougan went off by himself while Billy and Ralph took a

bar of soap and headed for the lake. Dougan came into the kitchen about 5:00 P.M. shaved and in clean clothes. Burt and Lizzy, the hired girl, were busy. "Anything I can do to help?" he offered.

Burt didn't look up. "Pack some water, fill the reservoir, bring in some wood and coal, peel the potatoes, milk the cow, gather the eggs and hang out the wash," she ordered sarcastically.

Dougan grabbed the milk pail and headed for the barn. He couldn't read Burt. Was she putting on a face for Lizzy's benefit or was she really being short with him? He didn't have long to think as Sandy accosted him.

"Well, Mr. Dougan, what's it going to be? Staying on the ranch and staying away from my wife or hitting the road?"

"I'm sorry for the misunderstanding. I promised that I would stay through harvest and I keep my promises,"

"Just so we're clear on this. I expect your usual good work and no messing around," emphasized Sandy. "We've got a lot of work to do and it starts bright and early in the morning."

"Yes sir."

Chapter XVIII

August 12, 1927. Clang, clang, clang went the triangle as Sandy summoned the crew for breakfast. It was 6 A.M. and the sun was just rising. The wind that blew all day yesterday had died down, the lake had a fine mist blending into its surface, and the rooster was crowing his heart out.

They ate a huge breakfast and waited for the orders of the day. Only Billy, Ralph and Dougan remained. The rest of the haying crew had been sent home. Some would be needed for grain harvest, but that was a few weeks away.

"Dougan, you and I will start tilling the far west strips. Burt and I have the tractors already there and fueled up. Billy and Ralph, clean up and put away the saddles and pack gear, then, when you're done with that, saddle Pedro and Punch. Drive the cattle from the west pasture down the coulee to the east pasture. They should move easily as they're looking for some fresh grass. If you're not back for dinner, you can eat later. Billy, you can drive Dougan and me to the field in the truck."

Sandy and Dougan filled their canteens, tied dust scarves around their necks and headed for the truck. It was going to be a hot, dusty day.

Billy was excited about driving the truck. He was being allowed to drive it home alone. He had been practicing shifting and double clutching. He couldn't crank it on cold days, but today it turned over easily and started on the first crank.

Sandy got in front and Dougan in the back. Billy had placed a cushion on the seat so he could see better yet reach the pedals. There was only a slight jerk as Billy let out the clutch. He "ground a pound" getting into second gear. "Try that again, only double clutch this time," coached Sandy. The gears slid together with only a click. As they drove along, Sandy had Billy try to hit or avoid rocks and holes. "You have to know where your wheels are. It may save your life someday and it will make the ride smoother for passengers, not to mention saving your tires and suspension."

"I'm trying, Dad," replied Billy as he pulled himself higher to see the tracks and ruts better.

They got to the field and the waiting tractors. Sandy reached over and gave Billy a pat on the shoulder. "You're getting to be a good driver. One of these days you'll have your own rig, too."

Billy waited until the tractors started and then he drove the truck back toward the ranch yard. He waved to his Dad, "I'll see you at dinner." Sandy was already starting around the field with Dougan about 50 yards behind. They both waved back.

August 2005

Bill Jones, age 90, was sobbing. "That's the last time I saw my daddy alive. I'm sorry, daddy, I shouldn't have told you."

David Jones held his father who was now quiet and exhausted. Bill went to sleep just as it was getting light. David said goodbye to Isabel and drove home. On the way home, he tried to make some sense of the story he had just heard. It had been a standard family story that Grandpa Sandy was killed in a farming accident in 1927. None of the other details were ever made known.

Bill Jones had held his secret for 78 years. He had lived with his guilt and protected his mother's reputation. He had shielded his sisters from any knowledge of Burt's romantic fling. He didn't even tell his grandfather who took over the fatherly duties after Sandy's death. It was painfully obvious how this had weighed on him and changed the course of his life. Now he was reliving the guilt, shame, and pain of that summer.

"Burt" Jones had gone on to manage the ranch, put Billy, Beryl and Betty through college during the depression, and become a pillar of the community. She never remarried. David had spent summers with Grandma Jones on the T-6 ranch and had listened to her tell of the accident. He had also listened to her recite poetry by the hour. He had often wondered why his father had chosen to live across the state and not come back to the T-6.

To investigate the story would take some detective work.

None of the principals were alive. Betty died in 1992, Beryl
in January of 2005 and Ralph Burton in 1996. W.D. died in
1933, Kyle Jones died in 1960 and Burt in 1965. Maybe there
were newspaper accounts, journals or memories of more distant relatives.

The *Choteau Acantha* newspaper accounts were the first
place to look. The first account detailed the funeral and the
accident. The second mentioned a coroner's inquest regarding
the death. Jack Dougan was considered a person of interest
and was questioned by the coroner and the sheriff. The final
determination was accidental death.

Was there any other place to look or ask? Ralph Burton
was certainly involved in the summer activities. Possibly some
evidence was in his records. Ralph's father, Will Burton, was a
compulsive journal keeper. His journals of that summer stated:

On August 12, about 7 P.M., a telegram was delivered
to me from Pendroy, Montana: "J.R. Jones accidentally
killed today. Funeral Sunday 2 P.M." I got in touch with
Gertie and Elizabeth (Burt's sisters) at Delhi who were
advised of his death. The next morning getting in touch
with Elizabeth found she was planning to go to Pendroy
but would be a train behind me if I should leave Waterloo
at 10:35 A.M. which I did, meeting Ellen and Ed (Burt's
sister and brother-in-law) at the Souther's home in St.
Paul.

Ellen and I arrived at Pendroy Sat August 17 at sun-
down. We were met by Ralph and Jack Dougan, the
hired man.

Minerva seemed glad to see Ellen and I and talked
much of her fine home and ranch, but could not be reconciled to the loss of Sandy who had given her all of these
fine possessions.

Will Burton's journal then gave a lengthy description of the funeral and the social gatherings afterward. He also recounted the accepted version of the accident. There were no revelations in the journal, but confirmation of the details of the funeral and accident. But what about Ralph Burton's records? Maybe he had written or spoken of the accident.

Norma Burton, Ralph's widow, resided in Clear Lake, California. David visited her there. She had a vivid recollection of Ralph's stories about his summer on the T-6 and added a few more details. Ralph had told of seeing Dougan and Burt in an embrace shortly after the funeral. Burt was crying and Dougan was comforting her. Ralph was so upset at the sight that he reported it to W.D. and Kyle. Ralph also recounted that he thought Dougan had some hand in the accident or even caused it. Ralph's photo album contained snapshots of the Jones family, the big red barn and haying crew. It also contained portraits of Minerva with her finger wave coiffure and her flapper dress.

David contacted Ross Jones, Billy's cousin and Kyle Jones' son. Ross was 10 years younger so had no recollection of the accident, but remembered his father discussing the accident. There were no written documents surviving.

David was still puzzled. What had happened to Dougan? Had Billy reconciled his feelings toward his mother? He hoped Billy would be able to answer those questions. He spent several long nights with little Billy Jones going over the story endless times. Even though the story was told and retold, it remained consistent and Billy continued to feel guilt and remorse with each telling.

"What ever happened to Dougan?," David repeatedly asked.

Billy finally remembered. "Dougan stayed on at the ranch and took over the harvest. He got the neighbors to help and managed to get all the crops in before the first snow in September. He conferred frequently with Mother. One day when I was in school, they say Grandpa W.D. and Uncle Kyle came to the T-6 ranch. Grandpa was wearing his .45 and Kyle had a rifle. They took Dougan away in the car. When I got home from school, he was gone. We never heard from him again. Grandpa told me we wouldn't have to worry about Dougan any more. Mom kept on crying for the next few months."

Bill Jones slipped further into his dementia. He often wouldn't recognize his wife or other loved ones. He forgot to eat. He became too weak to walk about or to raise a fuss. His bed side rails kept him in his "corral."

David sat beside his father and held his gnarled, bony hand. Bill rose on one elbow and looked right at David. "Daddy, I knew you'd come back. You promised to never leave me nor forsake me."

David held Bill's hand tightly. Through tears, he said, "Billy, it's not your fault, it's not your fault."

Bill relaxed and drifted away. He died September 1, 2005 at age 90.

Epilogue

Bill and most of the relatives on the Burton side died of dementia. All of Minerva's eight siblings died with dementia. Minerva herself died with dementia. Bill did not come back to run the ranch until his mother was so demented she couldn't run it. Even then, there were huge conflicts and strife over Bill running "her" ranch.

Ralph Burton died with dementia. Beryl and Betty died of heart disease.

Billy had an estranged relationship with his mother after his father's death. He buried himself in schoolwork and took every chance to get away to Grandpa's place. He loved the T-6, but couldn't run it in partnership with his mother.

He followed in his father's and grandfather's footsteps. He became a community leader, an innovator in scientific farming and livestock management. He also served as county commissioner, an elder in his church, and helped raise 46 foster boys. Shortly before he died, he gave the T-6 away to a home for at-risk boys and girls, The Yellowstone Boys and Girls Ranch.

The T-6 is now divided up into 160-acre ranchettes. There are no Joneses left in Montana.

Acknowledgements

Many thanks to all who collaborated in making this amazing story come to life; to my mother, Anita Jones, who helped me remember and describe all the details of ranch life at the T-6. She passed away February 28, 2010 at the age of 92, but was able to read, critique and enjoy the story in the month before she died. Next, heartfelt thanks to my wife who encouraged and supported my efforts in completing the story. Thanks to Isabella Hernandez who lovingly cared for Bill Jones in the last months of his life. Special thanks to my literary friends who proof read, edited and critiqued the production: Doug and Loris Puckering, Jack Groom and Sharon Jones Stewart (my sister). Finally, thanks to the 7 Lazy P Guest Ranch: Chuck and Sharon Blixerud, owners, Dave Hovde, foreman and guide, and the wranglers who recreated the mountain pack trip into Big River Meadows with me in 2006.

W. David Jones, January 2010

The author (right) and his son at Big River Meadows.

About the Author

David Jones grew up on the T-6 Ranch featured in the story. He attended Rocky Mountain College in Billings, received his MD at University of Oregon and practiced Internal Medicine for thirty five years. He is retired and lives with his wife Candy in Bellingham, WA. Since retirement he is busy building kayaks, writing, and enjoying his grandchildren. His next novel is a Christian medical thriller set in the San Juan Islands. Jones plans to write other books featuring characters from Big River Meadows.

www.ingramcontent.com/pod-product-compliance
Lightning Source LLC
LaVergne TN
LVHW051053080426
835508LV00019B/1842